Economic and Social Commission for Asia and the Pacific

Regional Shipping and Port Development Strategies

Under a Changing Maritime Environment

ESCAP/UNDP
MARITIME POLICY PLANNING MODEL

UNITED NATIONS

New York, 2001

ST/ESCAP/2153

UNITED NATIONS PUBLICATION
Sales No. E.02.II.F.21
Copyright © United Nations 2001
ISBN: 92-1-120081-4

This study report was prepared by ESCAP with assistance and consultancy inputs from the Korea Maritime Institute.

The views expressed in this paper are those of the authors and do not necessarily reflect the views of the United Nations.

The designations employed and the presentation of the material in this publication do not imply the expression of any opinion whatsoever on the part of the Secretariat of the United Nations concerning the legal status of any country territory, city or area or of its authorities, or concerning the delimitation of its frontiers or boundaries.

This publication has been issued without formal editing.

ACKNOWLEDGEMENTS

Grateful acknowledgement is made to the Government of the Republic of Korea for the generous funding of this study.

CONTENTS

TABLES

FIGURES

SUMMARY

STUDY OBJECTIVE

This study is based on the application of the Maritime Policy Planning Models (MPPM) developed and maintained by the Transport, Communications, Tourism and Infrastructure Development Division of ESCAP. Its objective is to provide a planning context for informed decision making by governments, shipping lines and port authorities in the ESCAP region. It does this by providing detailed, quantified and internally consistent forecasts of the structure of the maritime container transport system serving the ESCAP region through to the year 2011.

These forecasts cover three broad areas: the volume and direction of container flows, the shape of the shipping network, and the port facilities required to service the trade.

ECONOMIC ASSUMPTIONS

The currency crisis of 1997 brought an abrupt halt to the long run of rapid growth that had been enjoyed by a number of Asian economies. Although most economies have displayed considerable resilience in the aftermath of the crisis, growth rates during the coming decade are not expected to match the very high rates experienced the early 1990s.

Nevertheless, in all of the major Asian economies other than Japan, growth is expected to continue to exceed the world average. China will continue to be the growth leader in the region, but as the decade proceeds, the fruits of recent economic changes in India will become evident as the country enters a period of sustained economic growth. The economies of South-East Asia are also expected to record solid, if unspectacular growth.

SCENARIOS

It has become increasingly clear that there are no insurmountable technical barriers to the future increase in size of containerships. Concept designs already exist for ships up to 18,000 TEU. The limits to growth, if there are any, will be market-determined.

Nevertheless, there is a significant divergence of views amongst competent and experienced analysts as to how large containerships will grow, and how rapid the increase in size is likely to be over the next decade, and the issue of container ship size has become one of the most hotly debated topics in the container shipping world at the present time.

Some analysts take the view that the search for economies of scale is inexorable, and will drive vessel sizes up through 12,000 TEU and even beyond within the next decade, despite the challenges in terminal handling that will need to be overcome.

According to this view, the move to larger and larger ships, driven by an inexorable search for economies of scale, will continue and, if anything, accelerate. The need to maximize the utilization of these large vessel will in turn drive a radical reduction on the number of port calls on major routes, and feed the development of global mega-ports served by fully integrated global networks.

Other analysts point out that the gains from each increment in size grow smaller as vessels grow larger, and argue that we have already reached or surpassed the point at which additional feedering and inventory costs would outweigh any further savings in slot costs on main line vessels. According to this view, although vessel size will continue to increase, it will do so at a slower rate, as shipping lines try to balance the slot cost reductions available from larger vessels with the cost and marketing advantages of maintaining a wide network of direct port calls. Other pressures – notably environmental opposition to dredging and resistance to ever-increasing concentration of containers on the land transport system – will also tend to limit ship size growth.

The study seeks to add some light in this issue, and on its implications for the region. The MPPM model suite provides a tool that can be used to analyze the plausibility of these competing hypotheses. The interactive nature of the models allows the analyst to modify the shipping system of the future to reflect alternative futures. However, the cargo assignment procedures, which mirror the observed choices made by shipping system users, can provide feedback on whether the proposed services are in fact likely to attract the cargo volumes required to make them sustainable.

The 'base case' explores a relatively conservative hypothesis. This is that the growing demand for the carriage of containerized cargoes will be met by a continuation of the slow 'creep' in ship size similar to that which characterized the 1970s and 1980s. This is combined with an increase in the number of 'strings' (as each service offered by a consortium of liner shipping companies has come to be known) that are operated in each of the major trades. The number of ports included on each string is similar to the number included on the major services of today.

The alternative 'big ships' scenario starts from a different assumption. At the core of this hypothesis lies the assumption that the major carriers will attempt to exploit further economics of scale, and deploy vessels of 10,000-12,000 TEU on the major trade lanes. In line with current thinking of how shipping patterns will evolve if these very large vessels come to dominate, it begins with the assumption that these ships will operate on radically simplified routes, calling at only one or two ports in Asia. The sustainability of these services is examined, and the implication for the major trans-shipment hubs explored.

KEY FINDINGS

TRADE

The compound annual growth rate for global container volumes from 1999 to 2006 is estimated to be 6.5 per cent. This is expected to fall very slightly to 6.0 per cent per annum between 2006 and 2011.

As the level of containerization of the major trades approaches the practical limit, the rate of increase in containerization will tend to decline. The shift towards a greater proportion of high-valued commodities will also tend to dampen container growth rate.

Offsetting these influences, the container trades will be boosted by trade liberalization and an increase in the share of international trade that is represented by manufactured goods.

The net result is expected to be that container trade growth rate during the study period will be somewhat below the average growth rate of 8.4 per cent per annum that was achieved during the last decade. The average growth rate through to 2006 has been estimated at 6.5 per cent per annum. For the following five years, the growth rate is expected to decline slightly to 6.0 per cent.

Asia's share of containerized exports is expected to rise by 5 per cent points from 46 per cent of the world total in 1999 to 51 per cent in 2011; the share of containerized imports is expected to rise by a similar percentage from 40 per cent to 44 per cent.

Exports from North Asia are expected to grow more slowly than exports for the world as a whole, due largely to subdued growth in containerized exports from Japan. North Asia's share of imports is also expected to fall over the forecast period, but to a less marked extent.

Container traffic to and from other parts of Asia is expected to grow more rapidly than the world average. Expansion is expected to be particularly rapid in China, continuing the trend of the last five years, and solid growth is expected in South Asia. South-East Asia is also expected to increase its share of world container traffic over the forecast period.

By 2011, China will be clearly the world's largest container market, outstripping USA in both imports and exports. Chinese exports including Hong Kong, China are expected to exceed 28 million TEU, while imports will approach 20 million TEU.

China is expected to experience continued strong economic growth throughout the forecast period. Improvements in inland logistics will assist in transforming the economic structure of provinces that have hitherto been comparatively unaffected by the economic transformation of the last decade, increasing further the role of manufactured goods in trade mix of China. There also remains considerable scope for increased containerization of Chinese cargoes.

> *The intra-Asian trade will continue to outperform global container growth by some percentage points, recording an average of 7.6 per cent per annum over the forecast period.*

Intra-Asian trade enjoyed spectacular growth in the decade prior to the 1997 currency crisis, with growth average well in excess of 10 per cent per annum for a decade. The crisis brought a sharp reversal of this pattern, with an absolute decline in cargo volumes in the following year. Growth in the trade has now resumed, and the prospects for the next decade appear solid.

Fostered and supported by regional free trade agreements such as ASEAN's Common Effective Preferential Tariff Scheme (CEPT), strong growth of intra-Asian trade is likely to continue throughout the forecast period. On the other hand, the North American Free Trade Agreement (NAFTA), together with expected sound growth in manufacturing industries in Latin America, is likely to encourage a limited amount of substitution away from Asia in the trans-Pacific trade. The net result is likely to be a continuation of the trend – observable over the last decade – for Asia to become its own major trading partner.

> *Growth of trade between North Asia and South-East Asia is likely to be slow, with an expected growth rate of around 5 per cent per annum over the coming decade.*

This trade component, which was the star performer of the early 1990s, has been hard hit first by the slowdown in the Japanese economy and then by the 1997 crisis. There is as yet no sign of any sustained recovery in Japan, and without a strong growth in Japan this trade will continue to languish. As a result, projected growth rates for this component are expected to be below the global average for all container trades.

SHIPPING

> *There are likely to be approximately 330 vessels with capacities of 6,000 TEU and above that would be deployed on routes to and from Asia by the year 2006. Under the assumptions of the 'base case' scenario, this will grow to over 470 by 2011.*

By the middle of the forecast period, it is expected that mainline services that focus primarily on the key hub ports on inter-continental routes will need to operate vessels of this scale to be competitive. Large vessels will be deployed in three trade lanes:

the trans-Pacific, and Far East - Europe and North American Atlantic Coast services via the Suez canal.

> *Under the assumptions of the 'big ships' scenario, the domination of these key trade routes will be even greater, with a total of 490 very large vessels in service on these routes in 2011. Approximately 130 of these would be of 10,000 TEU or above.*

In the 'big ships' scenario, 'express' services with minimal port calls become a major feature of the Asian trades by the end of decade. This encourages the use of even larger vessels on highly streamlined routes between key hub ports.

> *Some of the streamlined routes appear to have potential in the Europe-Far East trade and on the Suez route to the US Atlantic Coast, while the trans-Pacific route appears less promising for streamlined very large ship service.*

Despite the very large cargo volumes that will continue to be available on the trans-Pacific route, it appears unlikely that many vessels of 8000 TEU and up will see service in this trade over the next decade. The longer distances on the Far East-Europe and North America via the Suez route make them more suitable for very large vessel operations. On these routes also, the inclusion of calls at Singapore (or Tanjung Pelepas) and a Mediterranean hub port would allow the vessels to access a number of major markets without significant deviation. It is therefore likely that most vessels of 8,000 TEU and above will be deployed on these routes.

> *Under the assumptions of the 'base case' scenario, trans-shipment volumes at the key Asian hub ports could reach a total of 64 million TEU by the year 2011.*

Although the 'base case' scenario includes a large number of new routes making direct mainline calls at secondary ports, especially in China, trans-shipment continues to play a very major role, accounting for approximately 30 per cent of total port container handling movements within the ESCAP region.

> *While, as expected, the increased use of very large vessels on the inter-continental routes increases the total trans-shipment market, the scale of this increase is modest: under the 'big ships' scenario, trans-shipment volumes are just 3 million TEU greater than in the 'base case'.*

The streamlined routes operated by very large vessels that are included in the 'big ships' scenario rely very heavily on feeding cargoes over key hub ports, and the number of containers trans-shipped is therefore greater in this scenario. However, the modelling suggests that, while such services may be viable, particularly on the Suez routes, they will not necessarily come to dominate the shipping system. The modelling work suggests that other more conventional services, offering direct calls at a wider range of ports using somewhat smaller, although still very large, vessels (in the range 4,000 to 6,000 TEU) can profitably co-exist with the large express services.

This moderates the impact of the new style of service on overall trans-shipment volumes.

PORTS

> *There is a considerable potential for the development of a substantial trans-shipment business at several new regional hubs: Busan, Gwangyang, Port Klang, Tanjung Pelepas and Shanghai.*

There are a great number of ports throughout the world that aspire to hub status, and most can claim some particular advantages which in the eyes of a port's supporters, make it particularly well-placed to fulfil the hub role.

Most of these aspirations are doomed to disappointment. The essence of a hub-and-spoke system is that there are very few hubs, and many ports relegated to secondary status on the periphery of the system. In the battle for hub status, there are two great advantages that are difficult or impossible to duplicate: a location that is directly on a major sea lane; and a dense network of established services that allows cargoes to move between a wide variety of origins and destinations. As most established hub ports possess both of these advantages, it is extremely difficult for aspirants to force their way into the first rank.

However, there appear to be several ports within the ESCAP region whose aspirations to become a major regional hub are realistic. The modelling work indicates that there will be nine global scale trans-shipment ports in the ESCAP region, each handling in excess of 3 million TEU of trans-shipment cargoes per year.

> *In order to handle the anticipated port container traffic in 2011, over 430 new container berths will be required in the region. To construct and equip these berths will require investment of around $27 billion*

The largest number is accounted for by China including Hong Kong, China and Taiwan Province of China, which will require over 160 new berths by 2011. South-East Asia's requirements are around 120 berths, while North Asia (excluding China) and South Asia will require around 90 and 40 berths, respectively.

The estimated $27 billion investment requirement include only the cost of developing the terminals. Substantial additional investment will also be required to secure adequate access to the terminals by road, rail and inland waterways, which will be essential for the effective distribution of containers to expanded port hinterlands. The additional costs of dredging, the provision of breakwaters and the establishment of land transport links and intermodal interchanges could easily double this total. Devising appropriate strategies to mobilise this investment will be a major challenge for the governments of the region over the next decade.

1. INTRODUCTION

1.1 Objective and Scope

The objective of this study is to provide a planning context for informed decision making by governments, shipping lines and port authorities in the ESCAP region. It does this by providing detailed, quantified and internally consistent forecasts of the structure of the maritime container transport serving the countries in the ESCAP region through to the year 2011.

These forecasts cover three broad areas: the volume and direction of container flows, the shape of the shipping network, and the port facilities required to service the trade.

1.2 Study Approach

The approach to the study comprised nine major activities:

A. Data assembly: The main data collected in this first activity related to the underlying economic and trade developments influencing containerized trade, container flows, sailing schedules for container shipping services, container handling capacity and planned developments at ports, and container handling productivity at the concerned ports;

B. Mini-workshop, to conceptualize the study;

C. Processing of the data collected under activity A with a view to obtaining a consistent set of data from which projections could be made;

D. Base case scenario development: This activity involved three distinct tasks, namely:

   (1) Preparation of container flow matrices for 2006 and 2011.

   (2) Preparation of a 'base case' container shipping network.

   (3) Maritime Policy Planning Model (MPPM) runs for the development of the 'base case' scenario;

E. The development of alternative 'big ships' scenario;

F. Scenario evaluation through the application of MPPM;

G. Presentation of the preliminary findings of the study at a series of country-level seminars in China, India, Malaysia, Republic of Korea, Sri Lanka and Thailand;

H. Refine of the modelling to reflect the views, information and feedback received from participants in the seminars; and

I. Drafting of the study report.

At each of the country-level seminars, representatives from the host country prepared papers which provided data and information regarding: the historical development of container flows through the ports of the host country; the current status of port facilities, port productivity and container shipping services; forecasts of container traffic; and proposed port developments.

This was followed by a series of presentations from the study team on the nature of the models used to produce the forecasts, the underlying assumptions that were adopted in applying the models, and presentations of the preliminary results of the modelling work. Delegates were then encouraged to comment on both the assumptions used and the outputs of the modelling process. Comments received were then used to refine the assumptions and modelling approach in order to produce the final study outputs.

1.3 Modelling Approach

The study is based on the application of the MPPM developed and maintained by the Transport, Communications, Tourism and Infrastructure Development Division of ESCAP.

The MPPM suite was consciously developed with an open architecture that encourages user intervention at all stages of the modelling process. In developing the models, ESCAP adopted the philosophy that the international trade and shipping system was far too complex institutionally and operationally to be reduced to a set of deterministic mathematical relationships. The fundamental strategy is to allow the modeller to input as much information as he or she believes can be reliably obtained from exogenous sources, and to present these to the models in the form of a hypothesis. Using these conditions as constraints, the mathematical relationships embodied in the models are used to fill in the gaps, to ensure internal consistency and to provide feedback on the credibility of the modeller's initial hypothesis and suggest directions in which it should be revised.[1]

This approach to modelling inevitably means that producing forecasts is time-consuming, and demands a high level of both modelling expertise and industry knowledge on the part of the modeller. But it also allows the introduction of a host of considerations that defy mathematical formulation, and hence can produce forecasts that are genuinely realizable future states rather than Utopian abstractions.

---

[1] For a detailed explanation of how this works in practice for the various model components, the reader is referred to the MPPM User Manuals available from Transport, Communications, Tourism and Infrastructure Development Division, ESCAP.

1.3.1 The MPPM Suite

Two modules of the MPPM suite were applied in this study:

- the Trade module, used to produce forecasts of containerized cargo on a region to region basis, and to partition these trade flows into port-to-port cargo movements; and

- the Liner Shipping Network module, used to heuristically design a shipping network capable of accommodating those cargo flows, to assign the cargo to the network, and to estimate the total costs of different shipping system configurations.

1.4   Report Structure and Contents

The full details of the forecasts produced by the modelling process occupy in excess of 50 Mbytes of disk space and would fill many large volumes if produced in printed form. This report does not attempt a comprehensive presentation of the study forecasts. Rather, it attempts to present the salient features of the forecast in a readily interpretable form.

This Chapter 1 provides an introduction to the report. Chapter 2 discusses some of the major changes that have occurred in the container shipping environment over the last decade. Chapter 3 is concerned with the economic growth context within which the container forecasts are set, and the magnitude of the increase in container volumes that this economic growth will bring. Chapter 4 is devoted to discussion of the model's forecasts on structural changes in trade patterns.

In Chapter 5, two different possible directions of evolution of the liner shipping system are investigated under two different scenarios, known throughout this study as the 'base case' scenario and the 'big ships' scenario. Chapter 6 discusses the implications of these changes for fleet requirements.

Chapter 7 examines the implications of both changes in trade and the development of the shipping network for the volume of containers that will need to be handled in the ports of the region. In Chapter 8, the report focuses specifically on those ports that will play a key trans-shipment role of the coming decade, discussing both the total forecast volumes and the markets that they are likely to serve. In Chapter 9, estimates are provided of the port facilities that will be required to meet the projected container handling demand, and the investment implications of these requirements.

The report rounds off with a brief look at some policy implications of the forecasts in Chapter 10.

2.   CHANGES IN INTERNATIONAL TRADE AND SHIPPING

The past ten years has been a period of great and rapid changes in the port and shipping industries. These changes have been felt most profoundly in the liner shipping sector, where containerization continues to make a vital contribution to the region's rapidly growing international trade in the globalization process. In this chapter, these changes will be reviewed in the context of the larger forces that have brought significant changes in the structure of the world economy. This chapter will also examine how shipping lines, governments and port operators have responded to the challenges and opportunities that have arisen as a result of these changes, and how these responses have in turn transformed the relationships between the various parties.

2.1   Changes in International Trade

It is impossible to understand properly the changes that have occurred within the liner shipping and ports over the last decade without understanding the context in which these changes have taken place. The fundamental underlying factor has been an increased reliance on international trade as the primary engine of economic growth and development. This is a major ideological shift: many economies have in the past pursued development strategies that have emphasized self-sufficiency and the protection of domestic markets. However, in the recent past there has been a growing consensus that the route to prosperity lies in integration within the global economy.

The establishment of the World Trade Organisation (WTO), with the prominent role it has subsequently played in the liberalization of trade, is perhaps the clearest and most important institutional outcome of this trend. However, the adoption by regional associations, including APEC and ASEAN, of policies that are designed to enhance trade between their constituent economies has played an important supporting role. Partly through such multilateral institutions; partly through bilateral agreements; and partly through unilateral initiatives, most governments of the ESCAP region have adopted policies that reduce barriers to both trade and capital flows.

While reduction of trade barriers has increased the volume of trade, relaxation of restrictions on capital flows has accelerated the shift from low to higher value commodities. Greater acceptance of foreign direct investment (FDI), particularly in manufacturing, has induced many global and regional corporations to relocated some or all of their production to countries with lower labour costs. This trend commenced with the relocation of simple manufacturing processes for low valued commodities, but has since progressed to manufacture of intermediate and higher value goods and components, particularly of electronic components.

The impact of these policy changes can be seen clearly in Figure 2-1. The rate of world economic growth fluctuated greatly during the port-war period: from around 6 per cent for much of the 1960s to a little over 2 per cent during much of the 1970s. However, from 1950 through to 1990 the relationship between economic growth and growth in the value of international trade stayed almost constant: the value of trade grew approximately 1.5 times as fast as the world economy. The last decade has seen a major change in this ratio: the value of trade is now growing at around 2.2 times the rate of growth of the world economy.

Figure 2-1: Relationship between world trade growth and world economic growth over the post-war period

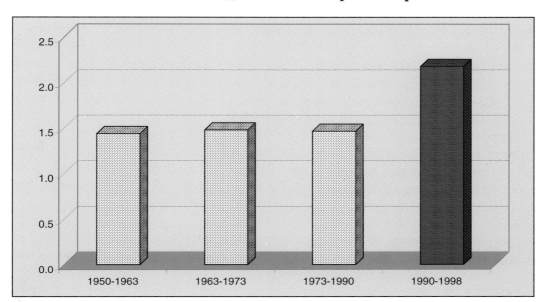

2.2 Competition and Regulation of Liner Shipping

While there have been important changes in the hardware of the liner shipping industry, especially in the size of ships, there have also been some significant changes which, although less visible, have been just as influential. This includes both the regulatory environment in which shipping lines operate and the way in which shipping lines themselves organize their activities.

To understand the changes that have taken place in the regulation of liner shipping, we must once again look at broader political and economic trends. Over the last 20 years or so there has been an increasing tendency towards economic liberalism in the shaping of industry policy, and there has been increased reliance on competition as the primary force of economic activities. Any industry structures or arrangements that are seen to diminish competition or interfere with customer-supplier relationships are seen as suspect in this environment, and the activities of shipping conferences fall clearly into this category. In line with this trend, governments have in general looked at the activities of shipping conferences less favourably, and sought regulatory changes to redefine the limits of collaborative arrangements between carriers.

2.2.1 United States

Under US legislation liner shipping activities that are deemed to be anti-competitive are listed. Those not listed are considered permissible. Prior to 1 May 1999, the relevant legislation was the *Shipping Act 1984*. After that date, competition policy relating to liner shipping was subject to the provisions of the *Ocean Shipping Reform Act 1998* (OSRA). Like its predecessor, the OSRA applies *inter alia* to common carriers, ocean freight forwarders and marine terminal operators.

The main features of the new legislation are:

- Under the OSRA, common carriers may enter into agreements to "discuss, fix or regulate transport rates, including through rates." Conferences and groups of ocean carriers are permitted to negotiate inland haulage rates or services with rail and trucking operators.

- Conferences must be open to new members, allow lines to withdraw without penalty, and allow any member to take independent action on any tariff rate or service item after giving not more than five calendar days' notice.

- OSRA applies to both conference agreements and non-conference co-operative agreements. The following types of agreement between non-conference lines are subject to the Act:

  - agreements to discuss rates and conditions of service;

  - agreements to pool or apportion revenue, earnings or losses;

  - agreements to regulate sailings or the volume of cargo carried;

  - agreements to engage in exclusive, preferential or co-operative working arrangements; and

  - agreements to regulate the use of service contracts.

OSRA differs from the *Shipping Act 1984* in several important respects:

- OSRA allows members of conferences and other forms of agreement to negotiate individual service contracts with shippers and their associations. This right also applies to unaffiliated shippers (i.e. shippers that do not belong to the relevant shipper association), which were previously unable to enter into such contracts;

- OSRA eliminates the obligation of ocean common carriers and conferences to file their tariffs with the Federal Maritime Commission (FMC). Whilst tariffs must still be made public in electronic form, FMC approval is no longer required before such tariffs can be implemented;

- OSRA reduces the information within service contracts that must be made public. Whilst contracts still have to be filed with the FMC, it is no longer necessary to disclose details of freight rates negotiated with individual customers;

- OSRA authorizes carriers to undertake joint negotiations with railroads, trucking companies and airlines for the inland transportation component of intermodal services; and

- OSRA authorizes the FMC to take action against the owners, operators, agents or masters of foreign vessels that exercise anti-competitive pricing practices.

In general, OSRA signals a move away from the tight regulation on liner shipping conferences in the USA towards greater reliance on market mechanisms. While anti-trust immunities remain in place, they are no longer buttressed by provisions that had the effect of enforcing pricing discipline on liner shipping conferences.

2.2.2 European Commission

Articles 85 and 86 of the EU Treaty are of the most direct interest and concern to liner shipping. Article 85 prohibits "any agreements or concerted practice between undertakings which may affect trade between member states and which have as their objective or effect the prevention, restriction, or distortion of competition within the Common Market." Article 86 lays down that "any abuse by one or more undertakings of a dominant position within the Common Market ... shall be prohibited ...'

Council Regulation 4056/86 provides block exemption for shipping conferences from Articles 85 and 86 of the Treaty of Rome 1957. Regulation 4056/86 states that exemption will apply only if the agreement, decision or concerted practice does not cause detriment to ports, transport users or carriers within the European Common Market. Detriment is deemed to exist if the rates and conditions of carriage applying to the same goods in the area covered by the agreement differ according to the country of origin or destination or the port of loading unless such rates can be economically justified.[2]

The last decade has seen two important developments in the European Commission's approach to regulation of liner shipping.

The first has been the ruling that consortia are not shipping conferences, and therefore do not enjoy automatic exemption from competition policy under Regulation 4056/86.

---

[2] The Commission has noted that external competition to conferences is an essential factor in the granting of the block exemption. Any restrictive agreements between conference lines and non-conference lines are therefore a cause of concern. OECD, Maritime Regulatory Reform – Comments by Delegations, DSTI/DOT/MTC(99)17, p.3.

As a consequence, the EC has introduced specific regulations exempting certain categories of consortia (EC Council Regulation 479/92 and Commission Regulation 870/95). Commission Regulation 870/95 included provisions for the monitoring of consortia based on market share. The market share of a consortium consisting solely of conference members is limited to 30 per cent, while a consortium of non-conference members is limited to a 35 per cent market share. Consortia that exceed these limits must notify the Commission. In the case of a consortium with 30-50 per cent market share, the Commission must oppose the exemption within six months failing which the consortium is deemed to be included under the block exemption. A consortium holding more than 50 per cent market share may not benefit from the block exemption. However, if the consortium is notified to the Commission and fulfils the conditions of Article 85(3), it may be granted an individual exemption.

The second is clarification of the European Commission stance with regard to the setting of intermodal rates. Whereas one of the major innovations of the US Shipping Act 1984 (retained in OSRA) was that it clarified the right of conferences to agree on inclusive rates for door-to-door movements, the EC has taken the view that conference agreements cannot include joint rate-setting for inland haulage.

The European Commission has noted that it is not at present considering any proposal to modify or abolish Council Regulation 4056/86 granting block exemption to liner conferences.[3] The Commission notes that it is focussing on clarifying the exact scope of the block exemption. Further, the Commission notes that it is strongly of the view that conference agreements should not impede the freedom of individual conference members to enter into individual and confidential contracts with shippers.

Nevertheless, the unmistakable drift of European policy has been towards limiting the scope of conference exemptions with the intention of enhancing the role of competitive market forces.

These developments in the US and Europe have clearly shaped the environment within which global liner shipping countries have shaped their strategies. This is all the more so as the regulatory framework within Asia is fragmented and generally places comparatively few restrictions on conference operations.

While these regulatory changes have been taking place, changes in shipping patterns and powerful new entrants have also eroded the power of traditional conferences. The expansion of feeder and relay alternatives to traditional direct shipping operations has undermined conferences ability to control capacity and rates in particular trade lanes. At the same time, several powerful new lines, in particular China Shipping Group and Mediterranean Shipping Company, have grown outside the conference system, while established non-conference operators, including Evergreen and Cosco, have maintained or increased their market presence.

---

[3] OECD, Maritime Regulatory Reform – Comments by Delegations, DSTI/DOT/MTC(99)17, p 3.

2.3   Shipping Line Response

The combination of these forces has created new and expanded challenges for liner shipping companies. Meanwhile, advances in global communications and logistics management have increased performance expectations of all transport enterprises.

Part of the response has been with new forms of collaboration, some broader and more diffused than traditional conference arrangements, others narrower and deeper. Cooperation between container shipping companies in many different forms of partnership such as slot purchase, slot exchange, vessel-sharing agreements or joint services has been an essential feature of the industry for a long time. These forms of carrier cooperation tended to be on a trade-specific basis. However, in recent years there has been a growing trend towards carrier alliances on a global basis. Carriers entered into partnerships that covered their operations worldwide – or at least on the main East-West routes – rather than on a single trade lane. This offered significant additional advantages in container logistics and the rationalization of port terminals, while allowing shipping lines to retain their distinctive marketing identities and ownership.

The latest development, however, has been a wave of mergers and acquisitions[4] that are clearly visible in statistics on the degree of concentration in the liner shipping industry. In 1988, the top twenty container lines controlled approximately 35 per cent of the total global TEU capacity.[5] This figure crept up, slowly but apparently inexorably, until by 1996 it had reached around 50 per cent of total global shipping capacity. Then, between 1996 and 1998 the share of the top twenty lines leapt to 70 per cent, as the merger wave began in earnest. In the last two years, there has been a further significant increase, so that nearly 80 per cent of total global capacity is now controlled by the top twenty lines (See Figure 2-2).

---

[4] Although the majority of the carriers acquired have been second- or third-tier operators, some significant carriers, including APL and DSR-Senator, were taken over by NOL and Hanjin respectively. P&O Containers and Nedlloyd Lines merged in 1997 to create P&O Nedlloyd Container Line, which later took over Blue Star Line and Tasman Express Line. Evergreen became the second largest carrier in the world, in terms of TEU slots under its control, through the takeover of Lloyd Triestino in 1998. In 1999, Maersk Line acquired the international shipping operations of Sea-Land to form a company controlling 9.2 per cent of the world container shipping fleet.

[5] Includes cellular fleet only.

Figure 2-2: Share of top 20 lines in total global capacity (1988–2000)

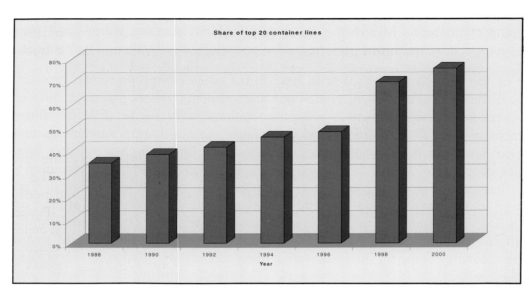

Source: Containerisation International, November issues, various years.

At the same time as they have been experimenting with new ways of relating to their colleagues, shipping lines have been desperately searching for ways to improve client service and to differentiate themselves from them. Some the major changes have been adopted by most if not all major lines into to improve service quality and lower costs. Larger vessels have been brought into service in order to reduce unit cost. Predictability has been enhanced by the almost universal adoption of fixed-day weekly services. The introduction of multiple strings on major trade routes has enabled lines improve transit times between important port pairs. Heavy investment in information technology and the use of multimodal services have reduced documentation and expedited processing.

However, the poor market conditions that dominated most of the 1990s convinced major operators that concentrating purely on the provision of line haul services on the sea leg was an inadequate business strategy. Essentially, this approach trapped the line into supplying a pure commodity that was easily replicated by competitors whenever markets appeared to be recovering, and lead to repeated entry and chronically low profitability.

The response was to seek ways to 'add value' through diversification and enhancement. Different lines have sought to do this in different ways. Many, led by the American lines, have sought to establish seamless intermodal services, extending their operations to include inland haulage and offering door-to-door transportation. Some, including P&O Nedlloyd, have developed other elements of the logistics chain, expanding their warehousing, cold storage and related activities. Most have taken advantage of more flexible regulatory regimes to move away from strict adherence to standard tariffs into price/service packages tailored for particular customers. Those lines with the capacity to do so have sought to negotiate global service arrangements with clients, protecting themselves by packaging a range of services that new entrants would find very difficult to emulate. Finally, many lines sought to improve the quality of the service that they offered to customers by increasingly sophisticated cargo care, improved information systems allowing continuous container tracking, and the introduction of a range of e-commerce initiatives.

2.4   Implications for Ports

As part of their response to the new challenges, shipping lines have also made greater demands on port facilities, in terms of both capacity and performance. The most obvious and frequently cited impact of the increase in vessel size is the need for greater channel depth. This is certainly a real issue. However, the post-Panamax vessels have tended to be designed in such a way that most of the increased capacity is provided by increasing the beam rather than the length or draft of the vessels: the first post-Panamax vessels were actually shorter than the first Panamax vessels, and required less draft.

The emphasis of greater breadth has, however, had important implications for terminal investment. Ports and terminals that wished to be candidates for calls by such large vessels have needed to acquire cranes that are taller with a longer outreach – and of course more expensive. This has been accompanied by an increase in the size of container terminals as the demand for land backing has risen in line with increases in vessel size.

Larger vessels also bring with them a need for better handling performance and container management in order to ensure that the time spent in port does not become excessive. This need is met in part by investment in increasingly sophisticated information technology system.

In the intensified port competition, international container terminal operators are extending the scope and scale of their activities and are operating terminals in ports around the world. Hutchinson Port Holdings (HPH), whose original stronghold was in Hong Kong, has developed a wide range of investments on the Chinese mainland, and has expanded its terminal operations to a total of 159 berths in 28 ports around the world. PSA Corporation of Singapore currently operates terminals in 10 different ports and continues to maintain its expansion strategy. Around 48 million TEU, or 21 per cent of the world container throughput, was handled at the terminals operated by PSA and HPH in 2000. Australian-based P&O Ports has a lower global throughput, but an even more diverse and growing range of port investments which includes facilities in China, SE Asia, India, the Middle East, Europe and Africa.

The developments of the last decade or so have seen a shift in the balance of power between shipping lines and ports – a shift in favour of shipping lines. The greater volumes that are now controlled by a single line or alliance mean that the capacity of an individual line to seriously affect the business of even a major port is now much greater than it has been in the past. The most dramatic recent example of course is Maersk Line's transfer of its business to the new port of Tanjung Pelepas. This decision of a single shipping line is expected to cost Singapore – the world's premier hub port – approximately 15 per cent of its total business. One of the main considerations in this and a number of other recent shifts is control – more and more lines are seeking dedicated terminal facilities and direct control over landside operations.

Finally, for most ports what comes in by sea must go out by land. Larger ships with faster discharge rates place increased stress on the land transport interface, and generate a need for faster and more efficient intermodal connections. These demands for enhanced port performance and increased investment in port facilities have in turn led to changes the port policy of many countries.

As a result we are seeing a change in the basic paradigm of port-carrier relations. The traditional paradigm is that ports serve basically local trade, and shipping lines come to the cargo. Under the emerging paradigm, shipping lines serve regional, largely non-local trade, and the cargo is moved – by feeder or intermodal service – to the ship.

Figure 2-3: Changes in international trade and responses of shipping and ports

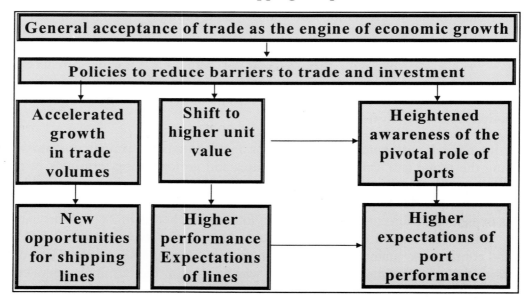

3. CONTAINER TRADE GROWTH

3.1 Background

During the 1980s and 1990s, international container trade continued to increase at a rate far exceeding that of maritime trade as a whole. Figure 3-1 shows worldwide growth in maritime trade volumes over the period 1987 through to 1999.

Figure 3-1: Growth of world maritime trade (1987–1999)

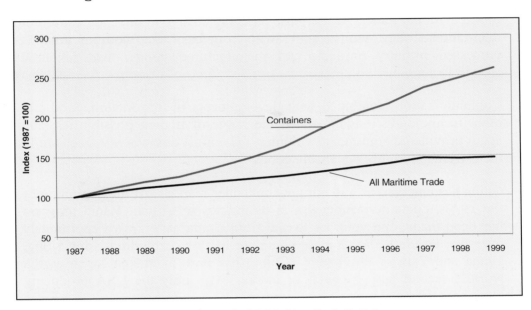

Source: Drewry Shipping Consultants; OECD Maritime Trade Statistics.

Total maritime trade volumes grew at an average of 3.3 per cent per annum over the period, with the result that, by 1999, total seaborne trade had increased by approximately 50 per cent over 1987 volumes. Containerized cargoes, by contrast, grew at an annual average growth rate of 8.3 per cent per annum over the same period, leading to an increase around 160 per cent in total maritime container movements. Due to the increasing importance of trans-shipment movements (the transfer of cargo from one ship to another) the number of containers handled in the world's ports grew at any even faster rate – in excess of 9 per cent.

During the 1980s, a large portion of the growth could be attributed by an increase in the container penetration rate. As more and more shippers became aware of the benefits of shipping in containers, and more and more ports developed the infrastructure and acquired the handling equipment needed to cater for container vessels, goods that had previously been shipped as loose cargoes gradually converted to containers.

Because this factor was so important, many commentators expected that growth in the container business would begin to slow during the 1990s. As the larger container markets mature – it was argued – the scope for further containerization would reduce, and the rate of growth slow to the much lower growth rates that had traditionally characterised the general cargo trades.

This did not happen, and there appear to be several reasons why it did not:

- As discussed in the previous chapter, liberalization of international trade and the globalization that has accompanied it, have accelerated the growth of international trade. At the same time, the change in the composition of international trade, with a shift away from basic commodities towards processed primary products and manufactured goods, also favoured growth in container volumes.

- Containerization, combined with developments in information, food and other technologies, has expanded the range of trading possibilities, and again provided a stimulus to volumes. The most obvious instances are in the carriage of highly perishable goods.

- China has emerged as a major new container market. At the beginning of the 1990s, containerization was in its infancy in China. Rapid progress has been made, and volumes to and from China have grown enormously over the decade. The Chinese container market (excluding Hong Kong, China and Taiwan Province of China) has now overtaken Japan as the world's second largest container market, with only the USA producing more containerized imports and exports.

3.2   Looking Forward

In essence, the trends of the last two decades are expected to continue. None of the forces noted in the previous section has yet run its course. Although current progress is disappointingly slow, a new round of world trade talks is still expected to commence soon, and this may well lead to further liberalization of world trade. Even without further progress, however, the commitments of the Uruguay round are likely to stay in place.   The growth in trade in perishable foodstuffs facilitated by containerization continues to be strong, and there are signs also of strong growth in containerization of some commodities for which container transport has not until now been considered a real option. A small but rapidly growing part of international grain movements, for example, now takes place in containers.

China is also expected to continue to be a major contributor to global container growth throughout the forecast period. Although some regions of China may now be regarded as mature, in many other regions – especially inland regions – the potential for further development is great. Moreover, there are other potential major markets, including India and Viet Nam within the ESCAP region and South America outside the region in particular, which have the capacity to provide a further major stimulus to global container volumes.

Over the next ten years, total maritime trade is forecast to grow at between 3.5 per cent and 4.0 per cent per annum – a slightly higher rate than that was experienced through the 1990s.[6] Although there is some variation between the estimates of individual commentators, expected growth rates for the container market generally lie in the range 6 per cent to 8 per cent per annum. Container growth rates are of course likely to be highest in less developed countries – such as China, India, Indonesia and Vietnam – where there remains considerable scope for the containers to increase their market share at the expense of more traditional cargo handling methods. However, even in those economies where containerization is mature, the rate of growth in container traffic is expected to exceed both the rate of economic growth and the general growth in maritime trade volumes.

3.3 Economic Assumptions

Growth in the container trade is ultimately driven by economic growth. An underlying assumption of this study is that, for the next decade at least, the structural relationships between the growth in container trade and economic growth will remain basically unchanged. The starting point for our analysis was therefore expectations of future economic growth.

The study has relied as far as possible on the projections of the LINK project – an ongoing joint research program between the UN and several universities – to underpin our estimates. The LINK project provides estimates for all of the major economies at the level of the individual economy, and also estimates for clusters of smaller economies (e.g. the Pacific Island states). It is therefore particularly useful for our purposes.

The LINK model projections however extend through only to 2004, whereas the study period runs through to 2011. In extending the forecast period, a very simple method was adopted in general: the average growth rate for the period during which the LINK project provided explicit forecasts was applied for the remainder of the forecast period. For some countries other sources available were also referred in estimating the GDP growth rates for the years beyond 2004. This was done for each economy independently.

The consequent economic growth estimates are shown in Figure 3-2. They embody a view of future economic growth that is reasonably optimistic. Since these forecasts

---

[6] Standard & Poor, World Sea Trade Service.

were prepared in the first half of 2001, the short-run outlook for the world economy has deteriorated still further. Japan's economy has suffered further setbacks, and is in technical recession; economic growth in the USA has slowed sharply; and growth estimates for some major European economies has been revised downwards by a significant level. It now appears that the world GDP growth forecasts for 2002, and perhaps also for 2001, may be optimistic.

Figure 3-2: Economic growth estimates underlying container forecasts

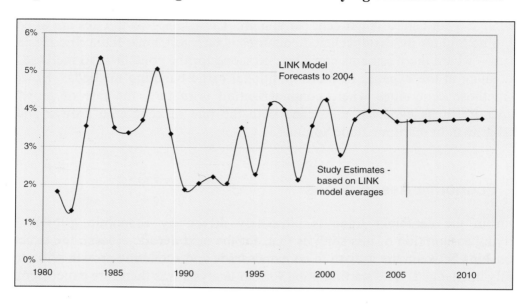

Source: Study estimates based on LINK Model forecasts, April 2001 and other sources.

The deeper economic slowdown will clearly impact on container volumes in the short term. It will not, however, necessarily invalidate the forecasts of this project. The horizon for these forecasts is medium term – 10 years from now – and although the timing of economic cycles during that period is impossible to predict, they will inevitably occur.

Figure 3-2 shows that the average growth rates predicted for the 2000-2011 period are consistent with the average for the previous fifteen years, if the major recession of the early 1990s is excluded. The economic growth assumptions underlying the present study may therefore be interpreted as hypothesising that growth will continue along a path similar to that of the recent past, and that, although there may be good years and bad years within the forecast period, there will not be a major, prolonged economic slowdown on the scale of that of the early 1990s.

Figure 3-3 shows a breakdown of forecast economic growth rates by region. East Asia, dominated by China, stands out as the area in which growth is anticipated to be most rapid, followed by the South Asian countries (dominated economically by India) and Latin America. South-East Asia is also expected to grow robustly, although at a more subdued pace than that experience prior to the 1997 collapse. The forecast also embody a positive outlook for the two regions that suffered the greatest economic difficulties during the 1990s: Africa and Eastern Europe. Western Europe, North America and Australia/New Zealand are expected to turn in very similar growth performances over the forecast period, while North Asia – which is dominated by the huge Japanese economy – is expected to experience somewhat slower growth.

Figure 3-3: Forecast GDP growth by region

(a) Within ESCAP

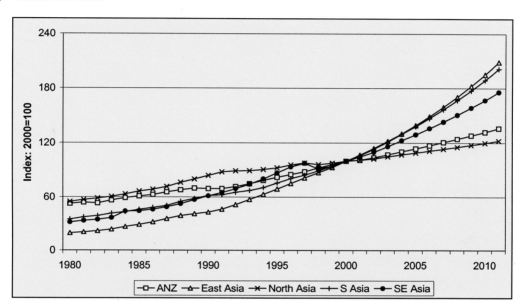

(b) Outside ESCAP

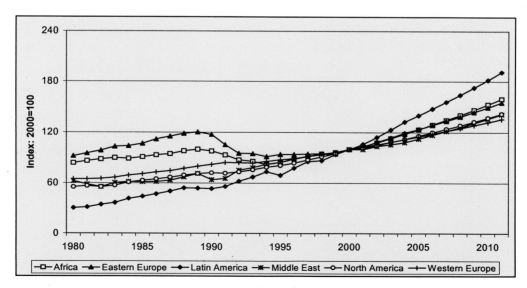

Source: Study estimates based on LINK Model forecasts, April 2001 and other sources.

The recent growth history and projected growth rates for the individual economies in North and East Asia, West and South Asia and South-East Asia are shown in Figure 3-4 (a), (b) and (c) respectively.

Figure 3-4: Forecast GDP growth rates of individual economies

(a) North and East Asia

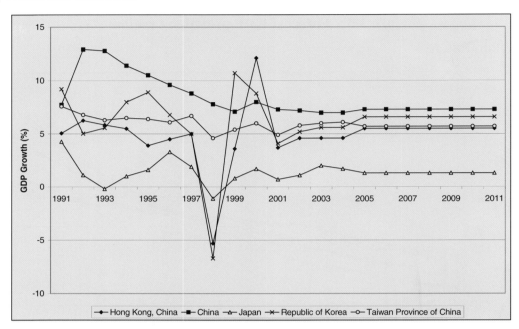

(b) South-East Asia

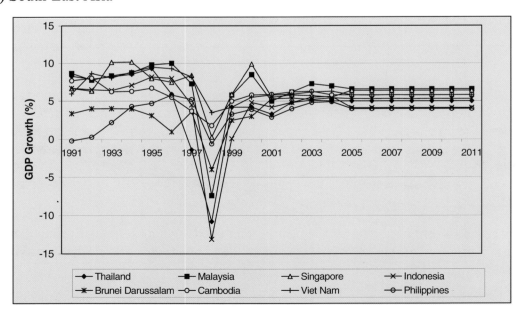

(c) West and South Asia

Source: Study estimates based on LINK Model forecasts, April 2001 and other sources.

3.4 Producing the Container Forecasts

The next step in the forecasting process was the conversion of economic growth rates into projected full container volumes. This was done by estimating separate forecasting equations for individual countries in the ESCAP region. For the countries outside of ESCAP, separate equations were estimated for each 'region', which was defined as a group of countries. Imports and export volumes were estimated from independent equations in each case.

There are a wide range of factors that impact on the volume of container imports and exports, including exchange rate fluctuations, changes in economic structure etc. However, for forecasting purposes it is necessary to use very simplified relationships, because many of the causal variables are themselves even harder to predict than container volumes. Container imports and exports are, for instance, undoubtedly greatly affected by exchange rate movements. However, the uncertainties involved in estimating exchange rates are immense.

The forecasting relationships that we have in fact used are simple, linear relationships between container volumes and GDP. In most cases, the regression analysis provided a surprisingly good fit for these simple relationships.

In a number of cases, however, the historical time series data was simply not able to support a formal regression process. This is the case in particular where the country is still in the very early stages of containerization — as in Cambodia and Myanmar — and where GDP data in convertible currency equivalent was unavailable — as for the Democratic Republic of Korea. In such cases, there was little alternative but to use professional judgement, informed by an examination of the history of containerization in similar countries during a similar phase of economic development.

3.5   Global Container Forecasts

Figure 3-5 shows the global container forecasts that result from this process. The volumes shown in the figure are full origin-destination containers only: that is, empty containers are not included, and each container is counted only once during its entires journey, regardless of how many times it may be handled.

Figure 3-5: Past and forecast global container volumes (1980–2011)

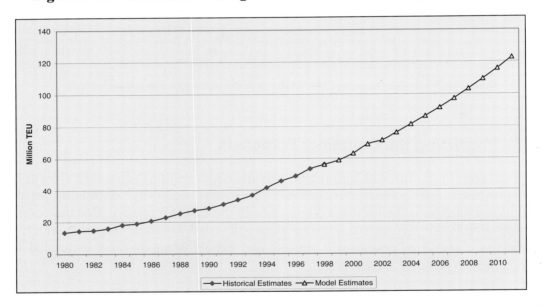

The total number of full containers shipped internationally is expected to grow to 122.7 million TEU by 2011, up from an estimated 59.0 million TEU in 1999, but at a slower rate of 6.3 per cent per annum compared to 8.4 per cent per annum that characterized the 1990s. Average growth during the first half of the forecast period is expected be sightly stronger than in the latter half: 6.5 per cent per annum is expected during the period of 1999-2006, falling slightly to 6.0 per cent per annum in the following five years.

These comparisons are summarised in Table 3-1.

Table 3-1: Estimated and forecast growth rates for container trade (1980–2011)

Year	Container volumes (million TEU)	Compound average growth rate over previous period
1980	13.5	-
1990	28.5	7.8%
1999	59.0	8.4%
2006	91.7	6.5%
2011	122.7	6.0%

Comparison of the study's forecasts with those provided by private consulting firms suggest that these global level estimates lie within the range of expert opinions, but slightly towards the more conservative end of that range.

It should be noted that these forecasts depend critically on the assumptions that are made about future world economic growth. Analysis conducted during the course of the study suggests that, for every 1 per cent per annum increase or decrease in estimated global economic growth, the rate of growth in container volumes will change by approximately 1.5 per cent per annum.

3.6 Geographical Distribution of Container Volumes

Figure 3-6 shows the estimated contribution made to total global container flows by each major geographical region[7] in the year 1999. The chart has been constructed by summing up the full import and export containers for each region, and computing the total as a percentage of total world imports plus exports. Figure 3-6 shows that Europe is the most import driver of the global container trade, generating 25 per cent of total trade, with East Asia the next most important region with 20 per cent of the total. North America generates a volume that is only slightly smaller, accounting for 17 per cent of the total trade. North Asia and South-East Asia account for 11 per cent and 10 per cent of global volumes, respectively.

Figure 3-7 indicates how these contributions are expected to change by 2011. By this time, it is expected that East Asia will have replaced Western Europe as the most import driver of the global container trade, although Europe will remain almost as important, with 22 per cent of the total. North America's share is expected to decline to 14 per cent, giving it only around two-thirds of the volume of the two leading areas.

---

[7] In this analysis, the countries in the ESCAP region are grouped into the following subregions: East Asia (China including Hong Kong, China and Taiwan Province of China); North Asia (Democratic People's Republic of Korea, Japan and Republic of Korea); South-East Asia (Brunei Darussalam, Cambodia, Indonesia, Malaysia, Myanmar, Philippines, Singapore, Thailand and Viet Nam); and South Asia (Bangladesh, India, Pakistan and Sri Lanka). Islamic Republic of Iran and Turkey are included in the Middle East, and Pacific Coast of Russian Federation is included in Europe.

Stronger growth over the period will also allow the volumes generated by South-East Asia to surpass those from North Asia, and Latin America and the South Asian countries are also expected to increase their share of the global total.

Looking closely at Asia, exports from North Asia are expected to grow more slowly than exports for the world as a whole, due largely to subdued growth in containerized exports from Japan. North Asia's share of imports is also expected to fall over the forecast period, but to a less marked extent.

Container traffic to and from other parts of Asia is expected to grow more rapidly than the world average. Expansion is expected to be particularly rapid in China, continuing the trend of the last five years, and solid growth is expected in South Asia. South-East Asia is also expected to increase its share of world container traffic over the forecast period.

Taken together, Asia's share of containerized exports is expected to rise by 5 per cent points from 46 per cent of the world total in 1999 to 51 per cent in 2011; the share of containerized imports is expected to rise by a similar percentage from 40 per cent to 44 per cent.

Figure 3-6: Distribution of container volumes – 1999

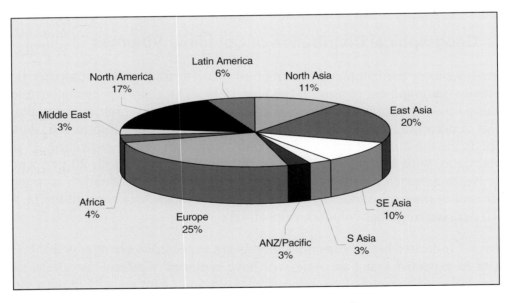

Figure 3-7: Distribution of container volumes – 2011

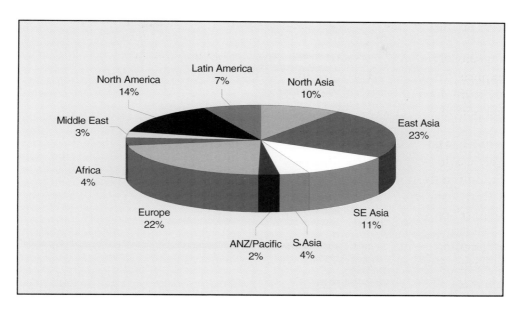

Forecasts exports and imports for the individual Asian economies included in the study are shown in Figures 3-8 and 3-9. The most notable feature of these graphs is the increasing dominance of China. By 2011, China will be clearly the world's largest container market, outstripping USA in both imports and exports. Chinese exports, including Hong Kong, China, are expected to exceed 28 million TEU, while imports will approach 20 million TEU.

China is expected to experience continued strong economic growth throughout the forecast period. Improvements in inland logistics will assist in transforming the economic structure of provinces that have hitherto been comparatively unaffected by the economic transformation of the last decade, increasing further the role of manufactured goods in the trade mix of China. There also remains considerable scope for increased containerization of Chinese cargoes.

Figure 3-8: Forecast container exports by individual economy – 2011

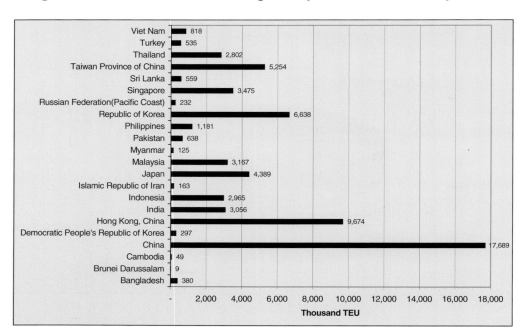

Figure 3-9: Forecast container imports by individual economy – 2011

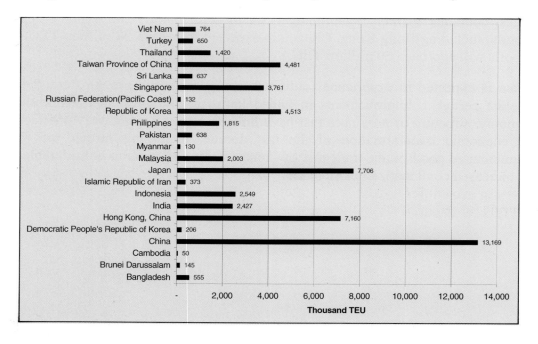

4. TRADE STRUCTURE

4.1 Changing Nature of Asian Trade

The growth that has occurred in the Asian economies over the last decade has brought changes in both the composition and the geographical structure of Asian trade.

The growth model for almost all of the principal Asian economies has been based on trade:

> *'The newly industrialised countries of Asia are outstanding examples of the success of outward-looking strategies for economic development. Rapid growth in manufacturing output and incomes has been closely tied to rapid trade growth ... resource endowment has dictated an obvious and binding rationale for outward-looking trade development strategies for the resource-poor countries of Northeast and South-East Asia, but other Western Pacific developing countries have adopted the same policy course. While China's resource base is large in absolute terms, its population density is on average high, and its commitment to modernisation has also substantially increased trade dependence'* [8]

The pivotal role of trade as the driver of Asian economic growth is expected to continue over the next decade.

This growth in merchandise trade has occurred at the same time as a burgeoning of FDI by the more wealthy Asian economies, initially Japan, but subsequently the Republic of Korea; Taiwan Province of China; Hong Kong, China; and Singapore, in manufacturing plants located in lower wage cost countries. This, together with trends in manufacturing processes that have favoured the two-way trade in components and sub-assemblies, led to spectacular levels of growth in the intra-Asian container trades during the early and mid-1990s. The 1997 crisis led to a sharp reversal of this trend, as recession and currency depreciations undermined the purchasing power of the key importing economies. However, a number of factors suggest that long-term growth prospects for the intra-Asian trade remain strong:

- Sound medium to long term growth prospects for most Asian economies;

- Close proximity of a number of economies at very different levels of economic development;

- The continued importance of more economically advanced Asian economies as sources of FDI for the less developed economies of the region;

---

[8] Peter Drysdale, *International Economic Pluralism: Economic Policy in East Asia and the Pacific* (Allen & Unwin: Sydney, 1988), p. 152.

- Regional free trade agreements such as ASEAN's Common Effective Preferential Tariff Scheme (CEPT).

On the other hand, the North American Free Trade Agreement (NAFTA), together with expected sound growth in manufacturing industries in Latin America, is likely to encourage a limited substitution away from Asia in the trans-Pacific trade. The net result is likely to be a continuation of the trend of the 1990s for Asia to become its own major trading partner. However, the study results indicate some moderation in the pace at which this trend is likely to develop.

4.2 Asia - North America

It is expected that the trans-Pacific trade will show the weakest growth among the three major Asian trades (namely, Asia-North America, Asia-Europe, and Intra-Asia) over the next decade. This is partly because the growth prospects for Asian trade with North America are likely to be comparatively subdued as the long boom in the United States ends and the full impact of NAFTA is felt. It is also partly because Suez routes will become more important in carrying this trade as southern provinces of China, South-East Asia and later South Asia provide a higher percentage of total cargoes.

Since the Asian crisis trade growth has been very unbalanced, with strong growth in the eastbound trade coinciding with a deep and protracted slump in westbound volumes. The recent slowdown in the US economy has seen a drop in eastbound volumes. However, the longer-term forecasts suggest that the current trade imbalance is likely to persist.[9] An average growth rate of 5.1 per cent per annum over the next decade is forecast for the westbound trade, compared with a growth rate of 5.7 per cent per annum in the eastbound trade.

4.3 Asia - Europe

The prospects for the growth of Asia-Europe trade seem somewhat stronger. Like the trans-Pacific trade, this trade has become seriously unbalanced since the 1997 currency crises. In the early 1990s, the volume of cargo carried in each direction in this trade lane was reasonably equal: although westbound TEU numbers exceeded eastbound by around 10 per cent, this was offset by the fact that eastbound containers were, on average, significantly heavier.

By 1999, this had changed greatly, particularly with respect to Asian trade with Northern Europe. Standard & Poor estimate exports from 'the Far East'[10] to Northern Europe at over 2.4 million TEU in that year, compared to Asian imports from Europe of just 1.5 million TEU.

---

[9] East-West trade cargo flow analysis *Containerisation International*, July 2001.

[10] This term is used by Standard and Poor to include all Asian countries east of Myanmar.

Once again, the study forecasts little improvement in this imbalance. Eastbound volumes, which showed virtually no increase over the 1990s, are expected to increase at an average of 7.7 per cent per annum over the forecast period – slightly higher than the global average. The estimated rate of growth for westbound volumes, however, is also 7.7 per cent.

It should be noted that these growth rates covers the whole of the Asia-Europe trade, including some very mature markets such as Northern Europe- Japan, which are expected to grow only slowly. Some other components – for instance, trade between East Asia and the Mediterranean, and between India and all parts of Europe – are expected to grow more rapidly than the rates quoted above.

4.4   Intra-Asia

Until the 1997 crisis, the intra-Asian trade had been consistently the most rapidly growing trade in the world for a decade.

In 1991, K-Line quantified the intra-Asian cargo flows between nine major Asian economies: Hong Kong, China; Indonesia; Japan; Malaysia; the Philippines; Republic of Korea; Singapore; Taiwan Province of China and Thailand. Total cargoes carried between countries/economies of the group at that time was estimated at 2.98 million TEU.[11] In April 1997, an attempt was made by DRI/Mercer World Sea Trade Service to quantify the level of trade between these same nine economies.[12] The estimated total for 1996 was 5.5 million TEU, a little short of double the 1991 total. This translates to a growth rate of 13 per cent per annum, compared to a growth in global container trade over the same period of around 8 per cent per annum.

It is likely that this quantification underestimated the real rate of growth in intra-Asian trade as a whole. The omission of China is the most obvious reason for this. In a separate publication, DRI/Mercer estimates that the number of containers flowing between the ports of China and the Far East Newly Industrialized Economies[13] grew at an average of 30 per cent per annum over the first half of the 1990s. The DRI/Mercer also omits other container markets that are expected to grow very rapidly over the forecast period: the most important of these are India and Viet Nam.

Although there is no question that this trade was hit particularly hard by the Asian crisis, it is difficult to obtain definitive estimates of the impact. Based on Standard and Poor's World Sea Trade Service data, it would appear that the trade was effectively stagnant over the period 1996 to 1998. However, the last two years appear

---

[11] The K-Line estimate is reproduced in Drewry Shipping Consultants, *Pacific Rim Trade & Shipping* (London: Drewry Shipping Consultants, 1993).

[12] This estimate is published in Intra-Asia - a trade that keeps on growing, *Containerisation International*, June 1997.

[13] Hong Kong, China; Republic of Korea; and Taiwan Province of Chian.

to have witnessed a return to solid growth, although at levels somewhat lower than those of the early 1990s. K-Line is just one of the major carriers reporting solid liftings, and a spate of new lines entering the trade also suggests an expanding market.

The study forecasts suggest that the intra-Asian trades are set for sustained solid growth over the next decade, with a compound average growth rate of 7.6 per cent per annum over the period.

Fostered and supported by regional free trade agreements such as ASEAN's Common Effective Preferential Tariff Scheme (CEPT), strong growth of intra-Asian trade is likely to continue throughout the forecast period. On the other hand, the North American Free Trade Agreement (NAFTA), together with expected sound growth in manufacturing industries in Latin America, is likely to encourage a limited amount of substitution away from Asia in the trans-Pacific trade. The net result is likely to be a continuation of the trend – observable over the last decade – for Asia to become its own major trading partner.

Within the intra-Asian trades, growth of trade between North Asia and South-East Asia is likely to be slow, with an expected growth rate of around 5 per cent per annum over the coming decade. This trade component, which was the star performer of the early 1990s, has been hard hit first by the slowdown in the Japanese economy and then by the 1997 crisis. There is as yet no sign of any sustained recovery in Japan, and without a strong growth in Japan this trade will continue to languish. As a result, projected growth rates for this component are expected to be below the global average for all container trades.

4.5   Minor Routes

Asia's container trade with Africa and Latin America and Australia is expected to grow at rates well in excess of the world average throughout the forecast period, averaging over 9 per cent per annum in both cases. This reflects improved economic performance and a greater acceptance of containerization in both of these partner regions.

By contrast, growth in the Australia-New Zealand trade is expected to be subdued, with an average growth rate of just 5 per cent per annum.

Figure 4-1 and Figure 4-2 show the implications of these growth rates for the geographical composition of Asia's container exports and imports respectively.

Figure 4-1: Origins of Asian export containers (1999 and 2011)

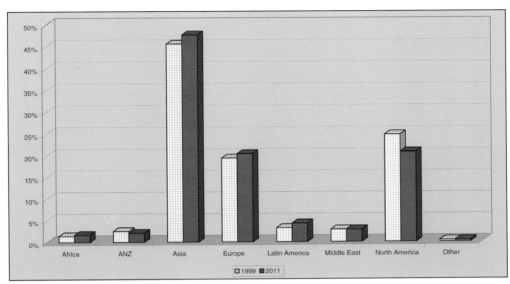

Source: Study estimates

Figure 4-2: Destinations of Asian import containers (1999 and 2011)

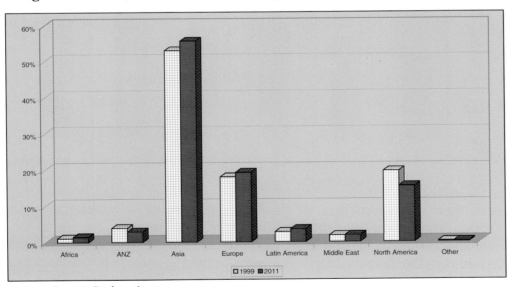

Source: Study estimates

5. THE SCENARIOS

5.1 The Issue

Increasing vessel size is not new in container shipping: a progressive increase in maximum vessel size has taken place throughout the history of containerization. By the mid-1970s, the 1,000 and 1,500 TEU ships of the first and second generation were being replaced by ships of 2,000 TEU-plus, signalling a trend of gradual increases that led eventually to the 4,000 TEU-plus Panamax vessels that most major lines were ordering in the early 1990s.

Figure 5-1: Increase in containership size (1976–2000)

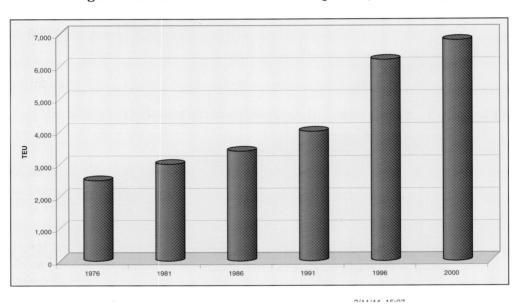

However, there was an uncharacteristically rapid increase in vessel size during the mid-1990s. This was due to the introduction of post-Panamax vessels in the liner trades. Post-Panamax is the collective term used to describe vessels that are too broad too pass through the Panama canal. The width of the Panama Canal was accepted as a constraint on container ship size until the late 1980s.

APL (now part of the NOL Group), which operated almost exclusively in the trans-Pacific trades, and did not use the canal, introduced the first post-Panamax vessel in 1986. This vessel had a capacity of 4,340 TEU. It was a few years before other shipping companies follow APL's lead, but, once they did, the full implications of breaking the Panamax barrier rapidly became clear. By 1996, vessels of around 6,000 TEU had appeared on the scene. Subsequently, we have seen a resumption of the 'size creep' that characterized earlier periods, and vessels that are formally rated at around 7,000 TEU are now in service.

It has become increasingly clear that there are no insurmountable technical barriers: concept designs already exist for ships up to 18,000 TEU. The limits to growth, if there are any, will be market-determined.

Nevertheless, there is a significant divergence of views amongst competent and experienced analysts as to how large containerships will grow, and how rapid the increase in size is likely to be over the next decade, and the issue of container ship size has become one of the most hotly debated topics in the container shipping world at the present time.

Some analysts take the view that the search for economies of scale is inexorable, and will drive vessel sizes up through 12,000 TEU and even beyond within the next decade, despite the challenges in terminal handling that will need to be overcome. According to this view, the move to larger and larger ships, driven by an inexorable search for economies of scale, will continue and, if anything, accelerate. The need to maximize the utilization of these large vessel will in turn drive a radical reduction on the number of port calls on major routes, and feed the development of global mega-ports served by fully integrated global networks.

Asaf Ashar of the US National Waterways Research Institute is a proponent of this view:

> *A convenient, although simplistic, way of describing the recent history of liner shipping is as one evolution and three revolutions.*
>
> *The evolution refers to the growth in size of the system's two major components, called hereafter as the 'duo': ships and ports. The revolutions refer to the changes in the system's linkages and the related expansion of its scope.*
>
> *The first revolution was in the ship-to-shore transfer, the invention of containers; the second was in the ship-to-rail transfer, the intermodal revolution; the third was in the ship-to-ship transfer, the trans-shipment revolution.*
>
> *This paper claims that the past model of evolution/revolutions will carry on. Accordingly, the long-term future of liner shipping is predicted to be shaped by a fourth revolution, this time in service or shipping pattern. This revolution is expected to be triggered by the expansion of the Panama Canal's locks. It will result in the emergence of equatorial-round-the- world (ERTW) services and a grid of supporting feeder services.*
>
> *A parallel evolution will take place in the system's two components, including: the emergence of new Panamax (NPX) ships with twice the capacity of the present largest ships, or 15,000TEU; and pure trans-shipment ports (PTP) to serve them, with annual throughputs of about 30-40 million TEU/year, more than twice the throughput of the largest ports of the present.[14]*

---

[14] Dr Asaf Ashar, <u>The fourth revolution</u>, *Containerisation International*, December 1999.

Others point out that the gains from each increment in size grow smaller as vessels grow larger, and argue that we have already reached or surpassed the point at which additional feedering and inventory costs would outweigh any further savings in slot costs on main line vessels. According to this view, although vessel size will continue to increase, it will do so at a slower rate, as shipping lines try to balance the slot cost reductions available from larger vessels with the cost and marketing advantages of maintaining a wide network of direct port calls. Other pressures – notably environmental opposition to dredging and resistance to ever-increasing concentration of containers on the land transport system – will also tend to limit ship size growth.

Martin Stopford, Managing Director of Clarkson Research, has recently presented this view persuasively:

> *... As the container industry matures, financial returns are elusive and management is responding in the way shipowners know best – a race for economies of scale.*
>
> *In the last few years liner companies have been consolidating at a tremendous pace and operators are funnelling bigger containerships into ever-bigger hubs. Already this year 105 supercontainerships have been ordered, and consolidation is the unquestioned king. However, there is a danger that the race for size could end up as a nasty case of middle age spread. Are big ships and bigger hubs really what inter-regional transport is about in the 21st century? ...*
>
> *Looking ahead, the consensus says that container trade will continue to grow at about 5% to 6% a year, which would triple it by 2025. ... If this trade is to happen, liner shipping must provide quality transport to each and every part of the world trade matrix, not just towns close to the arterial hubs. During the last 25 years, sea transport has become so cheap that distance hardly matters. The cost of shipping 15,500 bottles of scotch whisky from the UK to Japan has fallen from $1,560 in 1991 to $675 today. That works out at 4 cents a bottle!*
> *...*
>
> *However, in cluster trades, speed and reliability are crucial and rank ahead of cost. Supply chain management tops the agenda. ... Yet today's liner system seems to be going in the opposite direction. In their search for profitability they have a one-product strategy aimed at volume cargoes. Anyone who doubts this need only look at the WTSA's latest recovery plan, which targets wastepaper, soybeans, scrap metal and cotton for rate increases. This strategy demands ever-bigger ships in which every container gets treated the same. So far they have got up to 8,000TEU, but I keep reading about 15,000TEU container ships.*
>
> *Enterprising though this may be, it is a slippery slope. Containership operators are on the bottom cargo treadmill that hounded liner operators for a century. To fill the ship you must win more low value cargo, but to get the unit costs low enough to attract this cargo, you need even bigger ships and that in turn means bigger arterial hubs. Inevitably this slows the transit time,*

especially for the unfortunate customers at the extremes of the feeder network. That is fine for the lower value cargoes, but it will not suit the cluster cargoes, which need speed and certainty.

Nor does it guarantee profitability. It is surprising how slim the economic benefits of size become as you hit big-ship territory. Because ship related costs are less than one quarter of the total service cost, the financial benefits of size diminish rapidly as the ships get bigger. For example, ... on a 7,000-mile round voyage increasing the ship size from 4,000TEU to 6,500TEU ships only saves $46/TEU. If a feeder voyage is involved, that could add $200-300/TEU, dwarfing the saving on the deep-sea leg.

... The growth of the containership fleet has now created a clearing house from which ship operators can obtain ships on charter when they need them. Recently the containership fleet has reached 2,669 ships. There is now a thriving charter market where operators can obtain tonnage relatively cheaply. This will introduce flexibility into the system.

Pressure from the public and the environmental lobby will impose new constraints on the business that may well encourage direct services to local ports. In Europe and North America roads are clogged with lorries carrying containers. There will be mounting pressure to divert distribution of containers from land to a waterborne option.[15].

It would be going too far to say that these two views of how the liner shipping world will evolve are diametrically opposed. However, their difference is significant, and will have important ramifications for the strategies of both shipping lines and port operators over the next decade.

The study seeks to add some light in this issue, and on its implications for the region. The MPPM model suite provides a tool that can be used to analyze the plausibility of these competing hypotheses. The interactive nature of the models allows the analyst to modify the shipping system of the future to reflect alternative futures. However, the cargo assignment procedures, which mirror the observed choices made by shipping system users, can provide feedback on whether the proposed services are in fact likely to attract the cargo volumes required to make them sustainable.

A 'base case', which can be thought of as reflecting the Stopford view, is used to develop the core forecast. The alternative scenario, which we have labelled the 'big ships' case, is closer to the future as envisaged by Ashar.

---

[15] Martin Stopford, A new revolution, *Containerisation International*, January 2001.

5.2 The Scenarios

5.2.1 The 'Base Case'

Container shipping services to the region will clearly need to adapt to both the increased scale and the changing distribution of trade to, from and within the ESCAP region.

A close study of the existing shipping system reveals a complex mixture of a number of elements, including:

- Traditional end-to-end services calling at the ports in which cargo originates and discharging at the destination port, then reloading for the return journey;

- Mainline mothership services, focusing on global hub ports and carrying a high proportion of trans-shipment cargoes;

- Simple feeder services that carry cargo to these vessels; and

- Round-the-world, pendulum, and triangular services that serve a number of different trades sequentially.

There are of course a range of other services that do not fall neatly into any of these categories.

The 'base case' shipping system is based on the premise that this complexity will continue to be a characteristic of the liner shipping system through the forecast period. Essentially, it represents an evolutionary extension of the current shipping system. Adaptations were made to:

- Include additional ports as direct calls on mainline services where cargo volumes warranted (this was especially the case in China);

- Allow for an increase in scale of the largest vessels in service, up to 8,000 TEU in 2006 and 12,000 TEU in 2011;

- Add in additional strings and duplicate strings on mainline routes to ensure adequate capacity is available;

- Add additional inter-Asian service to enhance the inter-connectedness of the Asian port system (in keeping with the developments that have occurred over the last decade);

- Add new feeder services and increase the scale of feeder service to accommodate growth in secondary ports; and

- Include new feeder systems serving emerging trans-shipment hubs.

In summary, the 'base case' explores a relatively conservative hypothesis. This is that the growing demand for the carriage of containerized cargoes will be met by a continuation of the slow 'creep' in ship size similar to that which characterized the 1970s and 1980s. This is combined with an increase in the number of 'strings' (as each service offered by a consortium of liner shipping companies has come to be known) that are operated in each of the major trades. The number of ports included on each string is similar to the number included on the major services of today.

5.2.2   The 'Big Ships' Scenario

The 'big ships' scenario starts from a different assumption, i.e., that the major carriers will attempt to achieve further economies of scale, and deploy vessels of 10,000-12,000 TEU class on the major trade lanes. In line with current thinking of how shipping patterns will evolve if these very large vessels come to dominate, it begins with the assumption that these ships will operate on radically simplified routes, calling at only one or two ports in Asia. The sustainability of these services is examined, and the implication for the major trans-shipment hubs explored.

The 'big ships' scenario was developed by modifying the 'base case'. Hypothetical services using very large vessels (initially 12,000 TEU) were deployed on very streamlined routes between major ports. These streamlined routes include only one port call in North and East Asia, and where relevant one additional call in South-East Asia and (less frequently) a South Asian call.

The streamlined routes offered rapid transit times between the major ports, and in some instance allowed a weekly service to be offered with one less vessel than was normally the case. This, together with the economies of scale of the large vessels, significantly reduced mainline costs. On the other hand, as all cargoes for the service were consolidated in one or two ports, feedering costs were higher. The issue under consideration was whether the benefits would outweigh the advantages, and allow the services to be competitive when compared with more conventional services using somewhat smaller vessels and calling at a larger number of ports. (The scenario does not reserve the mainline routes exclusively for very large vessels operating streamlined services, but retains other more traditional services in competition with them).

The results of this experiment were somewhat mixed. On the trans-Pacific routes, a single port-to-port shuttle did not appear viable at any port. However, there does appear to be a possibility of a streamlined service collecting both South-East and East Asian cargo could be viable. The best routing for such a service appeared, perhaps unsurprisingly, to include Singapore and Hong Kong as the ports of call. If the restrictions of allowing only a single port of call in East Asia are relaxed, one or two other trans-Pacific services appear possibilities: in particular, the Hong Kong-Shanghai combination appears possible.

The Europe-Far East route appears more promising for streamlined large-ship service. This is particular so for services that include a call at either Colombo or Aden en route, and call at a Mediterranean hub port as well as a North European load center. While these may be departures from the pure 'shuttle' concept, there are still sufficiently streamlined to offer the possibility of providing a weekly service with just seven ships. In some instances, it is even possible to include a third Asian call.

A third route on which such services may be viable is on the Suez route to the USA. In this case, however, it is almost always necessary to include three, rather than two, Asian calls.

The final 'big ships' scenario, which presents a credible alternative hypothesis to the 'base case', is therefore something of a compromise on the original concept. The pure point-to-point shuttle concept does not appear viable for any port pair. However, very streamlined routes, combined one or two calls in East Asia with one in South Asia do appear to have some potential, particularly if other hubs can be included on a route with minimal deviation. This is the case in the Europe-Far East trade and on the Suez route to the USA.

6. FLEET REQUIREMENTS

6.1 Estimation Procedure

The Liner Shipping Network Module (LSNM) of the MPPM suite was used to obtain an estimate of the number of vessels required to service the trade task in the year 2006 and in 2011.

The starting point for the development of the future network was a detailed, route-by-route representation of the liner shipping network to, from and within the ESCAP region as it stood in 1999. Each mainline service, and many regional services, are individually represented in the coded network.

To arrive at an initial hypothesis as to how the 2006 network might appear, the capacity of the shipping network was increased by modifying the scale and frequency of particular routes. Certain structural adjustments similar to that outlined in the previous chapter (Section 5.2) on the 'base case' were also made to the network. The 2006 trade volumes were then loaded onto the modified network, and adjustments to frequencies, vessel sizes and ports of call were made, using an iterative process, until:

- a reasonable balance between supply and demand was achieved on all major routes;

- the specified frequencies and number of vessels on each route was compatible with model's estimates of the round voyage time, taking into account:

  - vessel speed and sailing distance,

  - the volume of cargo unloaded and loaded during the round trip, and

  - the cargo handling productivity at the ports at which that cargo is loaded and unloaded;

- box exchanges at key ports on major routes were reasonable; and

- the level of utilisation of the network as a whole, as measured by the global utilisation factor (GUF), was consistent with past experience.

The global utilisation factor is a statistic produced by the model that reports the ratio of slot-miles occupied to slot miles offered. It differs from conventional measures of capacity utilisation in several ways. Firstly, it reflects loadings on both the strong and weak legs of a trade route. Secondly, the study does not deal with cargoes whose origins and destinations both lie outside the ESCAP region, but a number of major routes with trans-Atlantic legs are included in the database for the MPPM runs. Thirdly, capacity utilization is usually measured as the number of TEU divided by the slots available on a trade lane. This provides an estimate of maximum utilization on a particular leg of a journey: it does not take into account the progressive reduction in load factor that can occur as a vessel proceeds through its discharge sequence.

Because the structure of the shipping network will influence the relationship between the GUF and utilization as normally measured, it is not possible to be definitive about the relationship between the two. However, past experience suggest that the GUF is significantly lower than load factors as conventionally measured, typically falling in the range 65 per cent to 70 per cent.

Once a satisfactory 2006 network was devised, the process was repeated in order to generate a plausible shipping system adequate to meet the demands of the 2011 cargo task.

The process described above is essentially experimental: it leads to a definition of the future shipping system which is internally consistent, compatible with estimated market demand, in line with known developments in the liner shipping world and reflective of many of the other, less readily quantified forces that shape the global liner shipping system. It does not, however, lead to a uniquely probable or optimal shipping network. This should be borne in mind when considering the results reported below.

6.2 Total Fleet Structure

If the 'big ships' scenario does eventuate, it will, of course, have implications for the size distribution of the container ship fleet serving the region. It will also have implications for both total trans-shipment volumes, and the distribution of trans-shipment opportunities between ports.

Figure 6-1 compares the fleet required in 2011 under the 'big ships' scenario with that required in the 'base case'. As the LSNM does not represent the small, semi-container routes that will continue to operate in the region, figures for vessels less than 500 TEU are not meaningful, and have been excluded from the analysis. [16]

---

[16] In simulating the shipping system, the MPPM suite uses a number of vessel archetypes, each of a standard size: 50, 100, 200, 500, 1000, 1500, 2000, 2500, 3000, 4000, 5000, 6000, 8000, 10000 and 12000 TEU.

Figure 6-1: Ship size distribution - 2011: base case and big ships scenarios

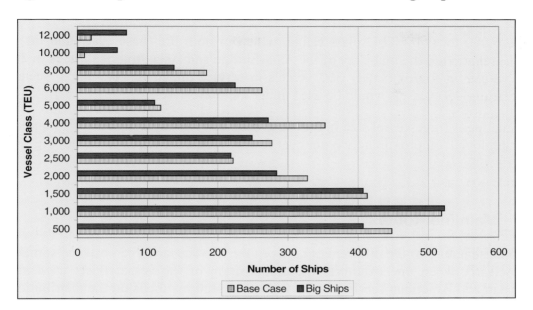

There are likely to be approximately 330 vessels with capacities of 6,000 TEU and above that would be deployed on routes to and from Asia by the year 2006. By the middle of the forecast period, it is expected that mainline services that focus primarily on the key hub ports on inter-continental routes will need to operate vessels of this scale to be competitive.

In 2011, it is expected that under the assumptions of the 'base case' scenario, over 470 vessels with capacities of 6,000 TEU and above will deployed on the key inter-continental routes to and from Asia, namely the trans-Pacific, Far East-Europe, and Far East-North American Atlantic Coast via Suez Canal.

In the 'big ships' scenario, 'express' services with minimal port calls become a major feature of the Asian trades by the end of decade. This encourages the use of even larger vessels on highly streamlined routes between key hub ports, and the domination of the key trade routes will be even greater, with a total of 490 very large vessels in service on these routes in 2011.

It can be readily seen from Figure 6-1 that the main difference between the two cases is the elimination of some of the smaller inter-continental services – typically operated by vessels in the order of 4,000 TEU – by the 10,000 TEU and 12,000 TEU ships of the streamlined East-West services. Approximately 130 vessels of 10,000 TEU and above, compared to 30 vessels in the 'base case', would be deployed under the 'big ships' scenario.

Under the assumptions of the 'base case' scenario, approximately 350 vessels with capacities of around 4,000 TEU would be deployed on routes to, from or within Asia by the year 2011, while under the 'big ships' assumptions only around 270 vessels of this size would still be used.

In the 6,000 to 8,000 TEU class range, which in both the 'base case' and the 'big ships' scenario are the mainstay of the Asia-Europe and Asia-America trades in 2011, there would be approximately 360 vessels in service under the 'big ships' scenario, while nearly 450 vessels would be used under the 'base case'.

The smaller average vessel size in the 'base case' is offset by a higher total number of ships deployed: approximately 6 per cent fewer vessels are required in the 'big ships' case.

6.3   Mainline Routes

The precise nature of the differences between the two scenarios can be seen somewhat more clearly when one examines the composition of the vessel fleets used in the European and American services. The following sections focus on the distribution of vessel sizes from the Northern European, trans-Pacific, and the United States Atlantic Coast[17] services respectively. The higher proportion of very large ships in the 'big ships' scenario can be seen clearly in each case.

Figure 6-2 shows the distribution of vessel size on the main line route between Europe and Asia. Although post-Panamax containerships were first introduced on the trans-Pacific route, in was on the Far East- Europe route that they first became the norm for leading consortia, and it is still the route on which most post-Panamax vessels are deployed. The model results suggest that this will also be the case for the largest vessels in the future. Of the 127 vessels of 10,000 TEU and above contemplated in the 'big ships' scenario, more than half are deployed on this route, contributing almost one-quarter of the total capacity deployed.

In the 'base case', this route is also dominated by very large vessels. More than half of the 520 vessels deployed on this route are of 6,000 TEU and above, and between them these vessels account for over two-thirds of total slot capacity. (In this scenario there are, by definition, few ships of 10,000 TEU and up: ships of around 8,000 TEU mark the upper limit for most lines).

---

[17] In the LSNM, most of the Altantic Coast services travel via Suez, and are therefore not constrained in size by the Panama Canal.

Figure 6-2: Distribution of vessel sizes: Northern European services (2006 and 2011)

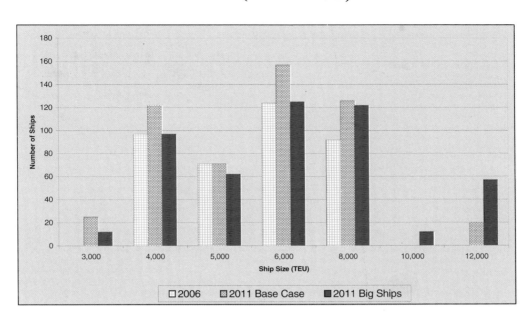

The other route on which very large vessels become attractive is the route from East Asia to the North American Atlantic Coast via the Suez Canal. In the 'big ships' case in particular, one service option that emerges as suitable for the deployment of very large ships on a streamlined limited call service is a combined service from Asia via a Mediterranean hub port to Europe and onto the US East Coast. The long sailing distance, combined with the very large volumes made available by jointly serving these two major markets, provide ideal conditions for the deployment of vessels at the top end of the size range. Most of the vessels dedicated to this service pattern, in either the 'base case' or the 'big ships' scenario, are of 6,000 TEU and above. The smaller vessels included in Figure 6-3 are largely from round the world services, which also serve the Asia-North American East Coast market but continue to be constrained by the Panamax limit.

This is in contrast to the size distribution of vessels deployed on the trans-Pacific route, shown in Figure 6-4. The modelling suggests that there are in fact very few services on the trans-Pacific route that could usefully be served by very large vessels. Generally, services connecting the major hubs on each side of the Pacific are well-served by vessels of around 6,000 TEU, and the modelling suggest that there will still be a great deal of scope for vessels of around 4,000 TEU on direct services connecting second-tier Asian ports to the key American destinations.

**Figure 6-3: Distribution of vessel sizes: Atlantic Coast services
(2006 and 2011)**

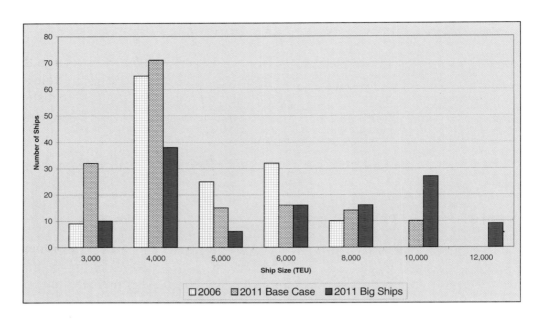

**Figure 6-4: Distribution of vessel sizes: the trans-Pacific route
(2006 and 2011)**

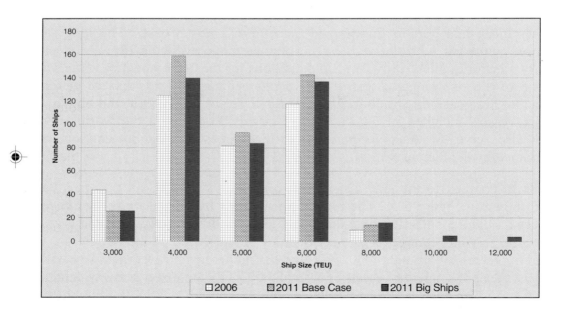

7. CONTAINER PORT VOLUMES

7.1 From Container Flows to Port Volumes

The forecasts discussed in Chapter 3 refer to the volume of containerized cargo that is shipped internationally. This information is difficult to obtain, and the values are subject to considerable measurement error. The most commonly quoted statistics on the size of the global container market refer to the number of container handling movements in ports, which is a more readily observable magnitude.

Port cargo handling volumes differ from the number of container movements because:

- Each container is counted at least twice, once at the port of export and once at the port of import;

- Some containers are trans-shipped at intermediate ports en route to their destination, is which case the container is counted twice more in port statistics: once as it is taken off the vessel and once as it is put back on;

- Port statistics also include empty containers loaded and unloaded in the port;

In addition, port statistics also include the movement of domestic containers, which are not included in the current study.

7.2 Empty Containers

However, empty container movements at present constitute approximately 14 per cent of total international container movements, and account for a significant component of throughput in most ports.

Excess capacity is likely to be a feature of liner shipping for the foreseeable future. This will continue to place pressure on operating margins, and provide a strong incentive for shipping lines to minimize logistics costs, of which empty container movements are a major component. At the same time, increasingly sophisticated container tracking and management procedures should provide opportunities for realizing economies in this area.

In the MPPM models, the approach to estimating the volume of empty containers handled in each port is simple. This approach is illustrated diagrammatically in Figure 7-1.

- The major direction for container movements is identified at each port: these may be either import direction, or the export direction.

- A percentage of empty containers is added to this major flow. The MPPM models have the capacity to vary this percentage from port to port. However, in previous studies we have found this to be a particularly unstable variable, and therefore difficult to predict with confidence. In this study, we have therefore chosen to apply a global average percentage to most ports: this was set at 3.5 per cent.

- Thirdly, the number of empty containers in the minor flow direction is estimated by subtracting the number of full containers in the minor flow direction from the total number of containers in the major flow direction. The assumption is therefore that total flows (full plus empties) are balanced in each port. This assumption is unrealistic with regard to any particular port in any particular year. However, given the difficulty of predicting the actual ratio in future years, the minor impact that imbalances have on overall volumes, and the fact that globally a balance must be maintained, the simplifying assumption was felt to be justified.

Figure 7-1: Estimation of empty container movements: MPPM models

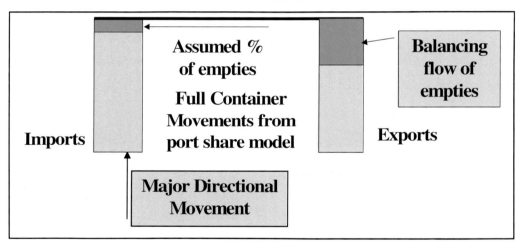

Figure 7-2 compares the ratio of empty to full container movements that results from this estimation procedure with changes in this ratio over the last 15 years. It can be seen that up to around 1996 there was a clear declining trend in this ratio, and increasingly sophisticated container logistics gradually reduced the number of 'unproductive' empty container movements. However, the last few data show a sudden upsurge in the percentage of empty container movements: this is due mainly to the emergence of very pronounced imbalance in the major East-West trades resulting from the Asian currency crisis, on the one hand, and persistently strong US growth on the other.

Our estimates of empty container movements in 2006 and 2011 suggest that the previous declining trend will plateau. They are consistent with the assumption that the recent increase is a transient phenomenon that will disappear as Asian and European growth rates recover, and the US slows, but that the significant reduction in unproductive movements that characterized the 1985-1995 period is unlikely to be repeated.

Figure 7-2: Empty container movements as a percentage of full container flows (1985–2011)

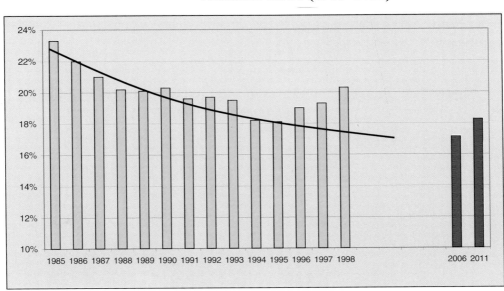

Source: Drewry Shipping Consultants (historical series); Study estimates.

7.3   Container Port Volumes: World and ESCAP Region

Containerisation International Yearbook reports that the total port handling movements in 1999 were 184.6 million TEU – that is, just over three times the total number of international containers shipped. Approximately 95 million of that total (52 per cent) was handled in the ports of ESCAP countries.

In the 'base case', the study forecast that the total volumes of international container handing in the ports of the ESCAP region will increase to over 155 million TEU by the year 2006, and by the end of the forecast period in 2011 the total volumes will have grown to around 216 million TEU. This implies an annual average growth rate over the period of 7.1 per cent per annum, which is somewhat higher than the rate at which the global containerized cargo market is expected to grow. Although the study does not produce explicit estimates of global port volumes, it appears likely on this basis that Asian ports share of the world container volumes will continue to grow over the next decade.

7.4 Container Volumes by Subregion and Economy

Subregional shares in the total container movements are shown in Figure 7-3. The two existing major hub ports, Singapore and Hong Kong, are reported separately.

The most obvious feature of the figure is the increase in China's share of total port throughput. To a large extent, this is simply a reflection of the expansion of Chinese imports and exports discussed in Chapter 3. This is buttressed by the development of a major trans-shipment business in Shanghai.

South-East Asia's share of the total market is also forecast to increase over the period, while the North Asian share is expected to decline. This is consistent with the trend of recent years.

Figure 7-3: Subregional shares of total Asian container handling movements (1999–2011)

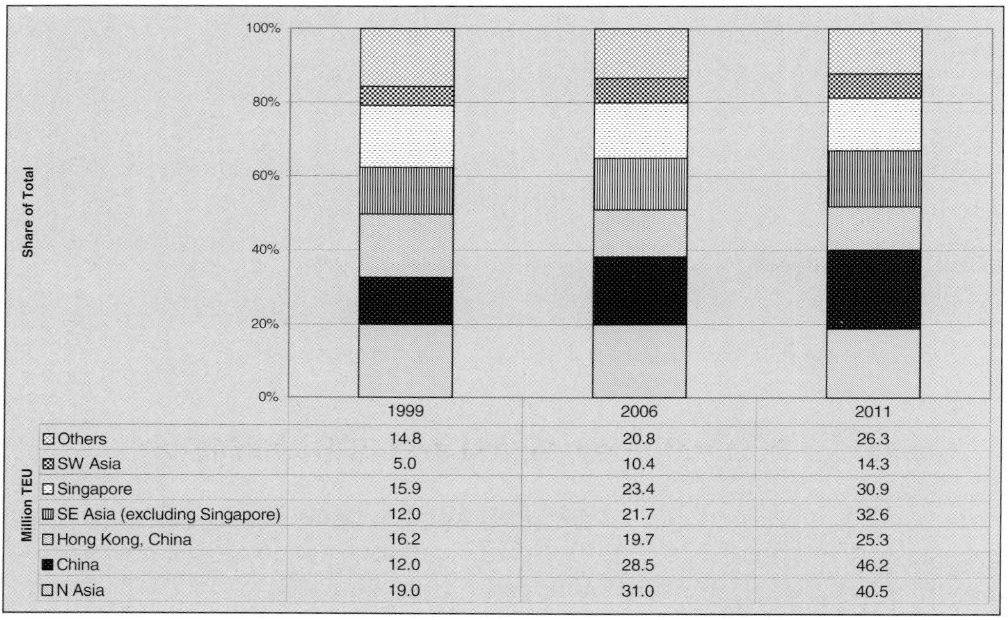

	1999	2006	2011
Others	14.8	20.8	26.3
SW Asia	5.0	10.4	14.3
Singapore	15.9	23.4	30.9
SE Asia (excluding Singapore)	12.0	21.7	32.6
Hong Kong, China	16.2	19.7	25.3
China	12.0	28.5	46.2
N Asia	19.0	31.0	40.5

Note: Others include Taiwan province of China; Australia and New Zealand; all Pacific Island country members of ESCAP; Turkey; and the Pacific Coast of Russian Federation.

A forecast of container throughputs of individual economies in the region is provided in Table 7-1. The most striking feature of the table is the increasing dominance of China, which is expected to be clearly Asia's largest generator of containerized cargo by 2006. It is estimated that the container throughput in the Chinese ports will increase at an annual rate of 12 per cent through the year 2011. China, when combined with Taiwan Province of China and Hong Kong, China, will account for 40 per cent of total container throughput of the ESCAP region. Among the East Asian economies, the Republic of Korea is also expected to experience rapid container growth, particularly owing to the emergence of the port of Gwangyang as a trans-shipment hub.

Another notable feature is the rapid increase in container handling in the ports of Malaysia, mainly due to expansion of the trans-shipment business. It is estimated that Malaysian port international container throughput will increase at an annual average rate of 12 per cent from 3.8 million TEU in 1999 to 14.6 million TEU in 2011, of which trans-shipment will account for 7.9 million TEU or 55 per cent. In the South-East Asia sub-region, high annual container growth is expected in Viet Nam (8.3 per cent) and Brunei Darussalam (14.0 per cent) from current low level of container penetration.

Countries in the South Asia sub-region are also expected to experience high increase rates of port container throughputs during the period from 1999 to 2011, i.e. 10.0 per cent in Sri Lanka, and 9.4 per cent in Bangladesh and in India.

Table 7-1: Forecast of port container throughputs by economy – 2011 (base case)*

(Thousand TEU)

Economies	1999 (CIY**/Other sources)	2006 (ESCAP MPPM)	2011 (ESCAP MPPM)
Australia	2,651	3,550	4,061
Bangladesh	392	770	1,151
Brunei Darussalam	62	188	300
Cambodia	n.a.	64	103
China	12,004	28,466	46,219
Democratic People's Republic of Korea	n.a.	161	614
Fiji	47	94	136
French Polynesia	31	137	189
Guam	123	223	284
Hong Kong, China	16,211	19,678	25,322
India	2,186	4,216	6,410
Indonesia	2,784	4,582	6,145
Islamic Republic of Iran	340	510	774
Japan***	11,503	14,307	17,087
Malaysia	3,775	8,444	14,556
Myanmar	118	182	270
New Caledonia	52	75	104
New Zealand	845	1,374	1,808
Pakistan	697	981	1,323
Papua New Guinea	138	215	291
Philippines	1,696	2,716	3,761
Republic of Korea	7,473	16,516	22,772
Russian Federation (Far East)	125	289	481
Singapore	15,945	23,393	30,940
Sri Lanka	1,704	4,447	5,372
Taiwan Province of China	9,758	13,245	16,874
Thailand	2,892	4,328	5,808
Turkey****	687	1,051	1,347
Viet Nam	653	1,185	1,701

*   Domestic coastal traffic is excluded.
**   *Containerisation International Yearbook*.
***   If annual 2 per cent economic growth, which is the official target of the Japanese economic growth from 2001 through 2010, is applied to the model, the projection for the year 2011 would be 20-21 million TEU.
****   Figure includes statistics from the ports of Mersin and Izmir only.

8.   PATTERNS OF TRANS-SHIPMENT

As size of container ships have increased, and the volume of containers have grown, container shipping networks have increased in complexity as well as in scale. The key development has been the evolution of hub-and-spoke systems with large mainline vessels serving a limited range of major ports to which cargoes are carried from tributary ports by feeder vessels.

Asia has led the world in this type of development. Singapore emerged in the late 1980s as the first port in the world that was dependant primarily on trans-shipment cargoes for its existence. Since then it has been joined by other ports in Asia, including Colombo, several ports in the Persian Gulf, and the new ports of Salalah, Aden and Tanjung Pelepas. In addition, a number of ports that have substantial volumes of hinterland cargo also play a major role in the trans-shipment system: these include ports of Hong Kong, Kaohsiung, Busan, Tokyo, and Port Klang.

Trans-shipment cargoes offer port authorities and terminal operators an opportunity to develop their businesses at a faster rate than the development of their economic hinterlands would permit. It is therefore not surprising that the competition for this business is fierce. However, as the recent decision of Maersk Line to move its South-East Asian hub from Singapore to Tanjung Pelepas has shown, it can also be very volatile.

It is therefore particularly useful to obtain some assessment of both the overall scale of this important market sector, and the extent to which individual ports are likely to be successful in it. The study has attempted to explore these issues. It should be borne in mind, however, that it is possible to do so only in so far as the competitive position of individual ports is determined by their quantifiable characteristics, such as location and cost structure. Policy variables, such as the priority that a terminal is willing to accord a shipping line or willingness to make dedicated terminals available to shipping lines, are likely to have an equally important bearing on eventual outcomes.

The study expects major changes in this sector, with patterns of trans-shipment changing rapidly as lines adapt their operating strategies to take full advantage of new opportunities. Well-established feeder operations in some areas will shrink, as volumes grow to the extent that large-scale direct services become viable. However, new opportunities will emerge as secondary ports that at present handle few containers begin to contribute to the feeder pool. This dynamic opportunities will offer opportunities for new emerging trans-shipment hubs: the study suggests that the new ports of Gwangyang (Republic of Korea) and Tanjung Pelepas (Malaysia) and the trans-shipment hub emerging in Shanghai will all capture substantial trans-shipment volumes. The traditional port centres of Singapore, Kaohsiung and Hong Kong are expected to retain their importance throughout the period.

8.1 Modelling Restriction and Biases

8.1.1 Restricted Trans-shipment

For technical reasons, the number of trans-shipment ports that can be included in the MPPM runs is limited to twenty. This is adequate to cover all of the major Asian hub ports, plus a representative selection of hubs outside of the ESCAP region that are necessary to preserve the connectivity of the system. For example, a trans-shipment center in the Mediterranean is essential in order to model the important option of trans-shipping cargoes from East Asia over the Mediterranean for the United States East Coast. The trans-shipment hubs of the outer Persian Gulf are also represented in the shipping network.

However, the limitation on the number of trans-shipment ports does mean that minor volumes of trans-shipment that take place at a range of ports such as Tanjung Perak, Manlia and Penang are not captured by the MPPM.

Figure 8-1: Trans-shipment ports included in model

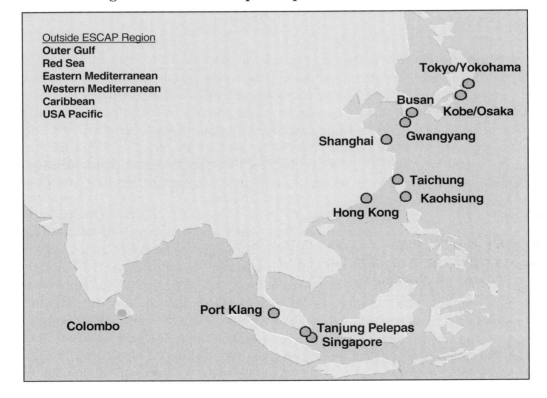

8.1.2   Omitted Routes

While the MPPM suite allows a fairly detailed representation of the liner shipping system, the network as presented by the MPPM remains a simplified representation of reality.[18]

This simplification has some consequences for the estimation of trans-shipment volumes. The MPPM requires that all of the cargoes generated in the ESCAP region are loaded onto the network. However, some of the smaller services – particularly those that carry a mix of break-bulk and container cargoes – are not included in the network. Therefore, where very small-scale or semi-container operations provide the only direct shipment connections between two ports, the simplified representation of the network in the MPPM cannot capture the direct movement of cargo between the pair of ports. The model must however find a way to reflect this movement, and this route is usually via a trans-shipment port. As a consequence, the MPPM has a tendency to overestimate trans-shipment volumes by a modest amount.

Past experience in using the MPPM indicates that this impact appears to be most pronounced at the ports of Singapore and Hong Kong, both of which are located in regions crisscrossed by networks of minor shipping services. In the case of these two ports, trans-shipment volumes in the calibration year were over-estimated by approximately 10 per cent.

8.2   Trans-shipment Volumes – Comparison of Scenarios

Figure 8-2 shows the MPPM's estimates for trans-shipment volumes at each of the ports within the ESCAP region. The study estimates that under the 'base case' scenario the total volume of containers trans-shipped within the ESCAP region will increase from an estimated 26 million TEU in 1999 to 47 million TEU in 2006, and 64 million TEU in 2011. The share of trans-shipment in total port volume is expected to increase from 28 per cent in 1999 to 30 per cent in 2011. These estimates reflect a set of assumptions that will tend to reflect the traditional role of hub ports in the regions.

The 'big ships' scenario provides a different perspective, sketching a scenario in which operators introduce very large ships on very streamlined routes. Such service will clearly depend very heavily on integration with a feeder network, and it was expected that the total trans-shipment volumes under this scenario will be correspondingly higher. Figure 8-2 shows that this did indeed prove to be the case.

---

[18] In the MPPM runs, the number of routes represented are 312 and 307 under the 'base case' scenario and the 'big ships' scenario respectively, although short-sea feeder routes are coded as a composite route with a single coded route representing the aggregate frequency and capacity of a number of individual services. In this respect, a 'route' is comprised of a sequence of port calls, and consequently individual shipping lines or consortia with similar sequences are combined to form a route.

Figure 8-2: Trans-shipment volumes in major ports: comparison of base case and big ships scenarios – 2011

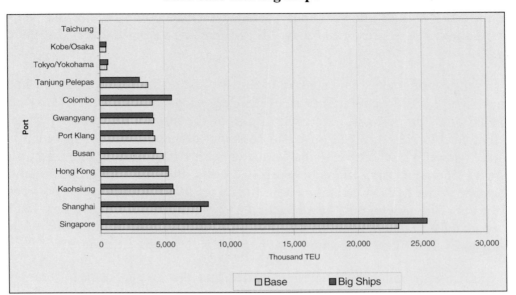

With respect to trans-shipment volumes, the most robust conclusion from the analysis is that Singapore is likely to gain significantly from the introduction of very large ships operating on highly streamlined routes. In part, Singapore's gain is at the expense of the trans-shipment business of its local rivals, Tanjung Pelepas and Port Klang, but is also in part due to a reduction in direct calls at other neighbouring ports, such as Laem Chabang.

In East Asia, the port most likely to gain under the 'big ships' scenario is Shanghai. The massive hinterland volumes expected at Shanghai by the end of the forecast period make it an obvious candidate for the single East Asian port of call on a streamlined service. As in the case of Singapore, some part of this increase comes at the expense of local trans-shipment rivals — in this case, Kaohsiung, Busan and Gwangyang. However, a reduction in the number of direct calls by major service at other ports of mainland China also contributes, with the result that increase at Shanghai exceeds the loss of volume at the other three ports.

Port of Hong Kong is also to command very large gateway volumes, and has a well-established trans-shipment role that could be further enhanced, although contrary to expectation the model estimated no gain at this port.

There also appears to be some potential for an increase in volumes at Colombo under the 'big ships' scenario. It should be noted that the model does not take into account physical constraints in the port: implicitly, it has been assumed that the dredging and other works required to accommodate the largest vessels will be undertaken. The model suggests that, as South Asian volumes grow, the additional of a Colombo call to services between Asia and Europe will become increasingly attractive to lines seeking to fill very large vessels on a streamlined service. The deviation involved in making the call is minimal, and provides access to a range of markets on the West Coast of India and Pakistan.

For the region as a whole, the trans-shipment volume under the 'big ships' scenario is estimated to be 4.5 per cent higher than the 'base case' by a total of around 3 million TEU per annum. The modelling work suggests that more conventional services, offering direct calls at a wider range of ports using somewhat smaller, although still very large, vessels (in the range 4,000 to 6,000 TEU) can profitably co-exist with the large express services. This moderates the impact of the new style of service on overall trans-shipment volumes.

8.3 The Major Trans-shipment Hubs

There are a great number of ports throughout the world that aspire to hub status, and most can claim some particular advantages, which in the eyes of a port's supporters, make it particularly well-placed to fulfil the hub role.

Most of these aspirations are doomed to disappointment. The essence of a hub-and-spoke system is that there are very few hubs, and many ports relegated to secondary status on the periphery of the system. In the battle for hub status, there are two great advantages that are difficult or impossible to duplicate: a location that is directly on a major sea lane; and a dense network of established services that allows cargoes to move between a wide variety of origins and destinations. As most established hub ports possess both of these advantages, it is extremely difficult for aspirants to force their way into the first rank.

However, there appear to be several ports within the ESCAP region whose aspirations to become a major regional hub are realistic. The modelling work indicates that there will be nine global scale trans-shipment ports in the ESCAP region, each handling in excess of 3 million TEU of trans-shipment cargoes per year.

8.3.1 Colombo

The MPPM forecasts suggest growth for trans-shipment volumes at Colombo: trans-shipment volumes are expected to increase fourfold to be in excess of 4 million TEU by 2011. At this level, trans-shipment would account for around 75 per cent of total port throughput.

Figure 8-3 shows that Colombo's trans-shipment business is generated by overwhelmingly Indian cargo. In 2011, almost 80 per cent of the total trans-shipment traffic through the port is expected to either originate in, or be destined for, an Indian destination. Most of the remainder is destined for Pakistan, Africa or the Persian Gulf countries, with a minor contribution from cargoes from East and South-East Asia relaying at Colombo on to services to the North American East Coast via the Suez Canal.

The dominant role played by Indian cargoes suggests that future trans-shipment business of Colombo is likely to be determined by:

- the growth of the Indian container market; and

- Colombo's share of that market.

With respect to the first of these points, the MPPM estimates are less optimistic than those presented in the previous study undertaken using the MPPM models. The 1997 study forecast a volume of 7.2 million TEU passing through Indian ports by 2006. This corresponded to an average growth rate of 16 per cent per annum. In fact, Indian container growth rates have been much more modest, and the 2006 forecasts in the present study have been revised downwards to 4.2 million TEU, rising to 6.4 million in 2011. However, it is acknowledged that there is substantial upside to these forecasts: Indian container volumes at present are well below those that could be expected given the country's population and per capital income. There is general agreement that the potential for containerization in Indian is vast: differences of view centre on how rapidly this potential will be realized.

**Figure 8-3: Breakdown of forecast trans-shipment movements:
Colombo – 2011 (base case)**

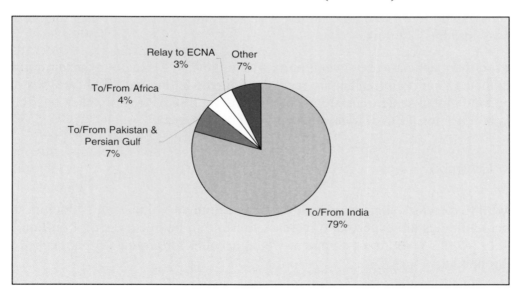

The forecast 3.2 million TEU trans-shipment movements to and from India corresponds to a 50 per cent share of the total Indian container market. While exact figures are not available, this is very similar to, although perhaps a fraction higher than, Colombo's current market share. In 1999, the volume of trans-shipment cargoes through Colombo was 1.15 million TEU, while total Indian container volumes in the same year was around 2.2 million TEU.

The key issue, then, is whether Colombo will sustain, increase or lose its share of the long haul South Asia market. In large part, this is likely to depend on port performance. If Colombo establishes and maintains a performance advantage, then it may be in a position to repeat in South Asia what Singapore has done in South-East Asia over the last fifteen years. In 1985, Singapore's total throughput was 1.5 million TEU. In the same year, the traffic generated in the other four large ASEAN countries, which provide the primary catchment for Singapore trans-shipment, was 1.95 million TEU. By 1999, the volume generated by these four countries had risen spectacularly, to 10.8 million TEU – more than 5 times the 1985 level. Singapore's volume, however, which was predominantly trans-shipment to/from these countries, had risen to 15.9 million TEU, or more than 10 times its 1985 level.[19] This is despite the introduction of direct mainline calls to ports such as Port Klang and Laem Chabang, and a rapidly growing trans-shipment business at the first of these two ports.

The study forecast could therefore be looked upon in the context of what might happen if everything went right for Colombo. However, Singapore's success has not been due to the rapid subregional growth and a fortunate location alone: it has been founded also on the ability of the port to deliver a very high level of performance at a modest cost. For Colombo to emulate the performance of Singapore in this regard will be extremely difficult. This is not only because of the intrinsic difficulty of achieving at this level. It is also because changes in the international port industry over the last decade have made world class expertise and investment capital more readily available than they were in the 1980s. As a consequence, it will be much more difficult for Colombo to create a sustainable performance advantage over Indian ports seeking to foster direct shipment of Indian cargoes. There is also the question of whether it is practical to expand the port capacity at Colombo at the rate that would be required to deal with this level of growth.

Competition from other alternative trans-shipment ports will also be an important factor. Several Indian ports, including Chennai, Cochin and Tuticorin have proclaimed ambitions to become a hub port for Indian cargoes. Aden also provides an attractive alternative for linking these regions to the global shipping system. Realising potential trans-shipment volumes at Colombo will therefore be more than usually sensitive to port performance and productivity.

8.3.2 Port Kelang

Trans-shipment at Port Kelang, has increased rapidly over the last few years, due in part to a concerted campaign by the Malaysian government and terminal operators to attract trans-shipment business. This campaign included a 50 per cent reduction in

---

[19] These volumes are based on data from *Containerisation International Yearbook*, various issues.

charges for trans-shipment containers – charges which were already very low by international standards.

The total predicted trans-shipment volume at Port Klang is 4.2 million TEU in 2011 under the 'base case'. In the 'big ships' scenario, predicted volumes are slightly lower, as mainline calls are more intensely concentrated on Singapore.

The MPPM suggests that the most important sources of trans-shipment cargoes for Port Klang are likely to be:

- cargoes from Sumatra to a wide range of destinations;

- cargoes from the Bay of Bengal to East Asia and the West Coast of North America;

- cargoes from Australia and New Zealand to Europe and South-East Asia; and

- cargoes from West India and the Gulf for South-East and East Asia, and to the US Pacific coast.

Figure 8-4:   **Breakdown of forecast trans-shipment movements: Port Klang – 2011 (base case)**

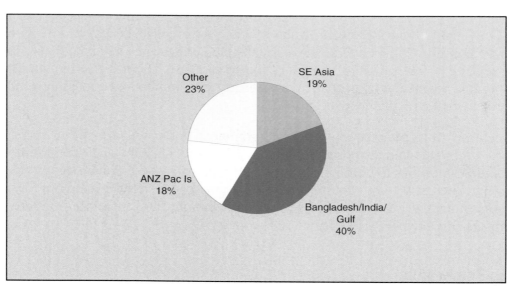

It is worth noting that the composition of forecast trans-shipment volumes at Port Klang is significantly different from Singapore. South-East Asia feeder cargoes, especially from the Thai and Javanese ports that are of crucial importance to Singapore, are not so important to Port Klang. This is not surprising, as cargoes from these markets must pass by Singapore if it is to be trans-shipped in Port Klang. On the other hand, Port Klang is strongly supported by Sumatran cargoes, cargoes from the Bay of Bengal; less obviously, the model suggests considerable potential as a relay port for cargoes from other parts of the subcontinent and from the Persian Gulf.

8.3.3 Singapore

In both scenarios, Singapore continues to dominate the South-East Asian trans-shipment sector.

Not surprisingly, Singapore projections are very sensitive to the assumptions that are made about structural developments in the shipping system. Under the 'base case' scenario assumptions, the total predicted trans-shipment volume at Singapore in 2011 is 23.1 million TEU, but this rises to 25.4 million TEU under the 'big ships' scenario.

Cargoes originating in or bound for South-East Asia will continue to dominate trans-shipment through Singapore. In the 'base case' scenario, it is estimated that nearly 70 per cent of total trans-shipment cargoes through Singapore will have a South-East Asian origin or destination. Other important markets in the 'base case' scenario are Bangladeshi, Indian and Middle Eastern cargoes bound for East Asia and the West Coast of North America.

Figure 8-5: Breakdown of forecast trans-shipment movements: Singapore – 2011 (base case)

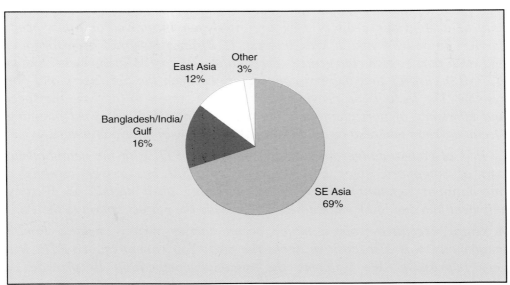

8.3.4 Tanjung Pelepas

The new Malaysian port of Tanjung Pelepas caused a major sensation in the liner shipping world during 2000 when Maersk Line announced its intention to transfer most of its major services to the port from Singapore. Maersk Line later took a substantial equity stake in the port.

The sensation caused by this event was due only in part to magnitude of the volume that Maersk commanded. It was also due in part to the realization that, after two decades in which Singapore's pre-eminence as a hub port had been essentially unchallenged, a major global carrier took the view that a genuine alternative was possible.

> *All the facilities are new and state of the art, and as a green field site, the opportunity for development is immense.*
>
> *What exactly does Tanjung Pelepas have to offer? The major selling points of the port are that it is new, it is flexible, it has state of the art facilities, good financial backing, room to expand, an ability to cater for post-Panamax vessels, warehousing facilities, IT systems, hinterland links and an initial base cargo. It can also offer cost savings. Not a bad CV for such a new, untested port. ... Sidik [CEO of Tanjung Pelepas] was eager to labour the positive points and claimed: In terms of location, it is second to none and is comparable geographically to Singapore. We do not have a legacy, we do not have something on the established procedures of how we work. Shipping lines tell us how they want us to work. We are flexible and we do not have unions.*
>
> *The facilities are also important, and the number of berths and cranes and natural deep water draft of 15m are surely an incentive for other ocean carriers to at least take a keen interest. IT systems have not been forgotten and the port's own Integrated Terminal and Port Management System (ITPMIS) ensures that there is connectivity between the port users and port systems. The focus is on providing a paperless system to increase the speed and efficiency of port clearance, berth allocation, ship and yard planning. Ocean carriers will also be able to manage the flow of their containers.*
>
> *... It is of course dangerous to start comparing PTP with the neighbouring port of Singapore, since PSA Corporation (PSA) has a well established international reputation, but PTP is marketing itself mainly as a transshipment hub and Sidik maintained: We provide the perfect option to the PSA.*
>
> *A senior executive from a major ocean carrier who wished to remain anonymous, was also positive about the port: You cannot ignore PTP. It is very impressive. We welcome the regional competition to provide an alternative in Malaysia. It may push the PSA to become more competitive. Customers want the best service at the best price. Perhaps it is wrong to compare Tanjung Pelepas to Singapore at such an embryonic stage of the former's development, although the comparison is inevitable. However, ... then the PSA and neighbouring ports should take note that there is another*

major player in South East Asia that is quickly gaining the attention of carriers and manufacturers alike. The port has a lot of hard work to do, but everything is geared to the future and capitalising on expected trade growth. Also, the port has the ability to expand and adapt. Tanjung Pelepas's David may not be able to smite Singapore's mighty Goliath, but it seems set to give it a run for its money[20].

The longer-term prospects for the port have since been the subject of considerable debate in trade press, and views expressed at the Malaysian country workshop were by no means uniform.

The modelling work undertaken for the present study suggests that Tanjung Pelepas has the potential to build a very strong trans-shipment business, although it is unlikely to pose a major threat to the dominance of Singapore within the forecast period. Under the assumptions of the 'base case', throughput at Tanjung Pelepas is expected to grow to 4.5 million TEU by 2011, over 80 per cent of which will be trans-shipment cargoes.

The positioning of Tanjung Pelepas as a head-to-head competitor of Singapore is underscored by similarities in the composition of their trans-shipment cargoes. Tanjung Pelepas is also very heavily dependant on the South-East Asian market – even more so, in fact, than Singapore. It is estimated that South-East Asian traffic will account for 86 per cent of Tanjung Pelepas total trans-shipment traffic in 2011.

Figure 8-6: Breakdown of forecast trans-shipment movements: Tanjung Pelepas – 2011 (base case)

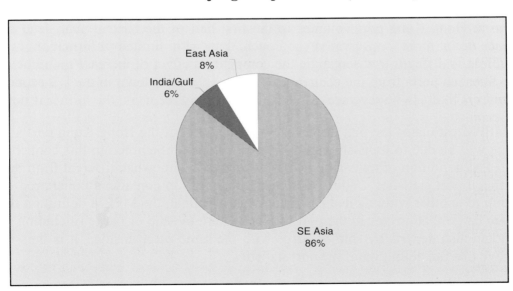

---

[20] <u>David and Goliath</u>, *Containerisation International*, December 2000.

8.3.5   Hong Kong, China

The MPPM estimate of the Hong Kong port's volume in 2011 is 25.3 million TEU under the 'base case' scenario. Somewhat surprisingly, estimated volumes are almost precisely the same under the 'big ships' scenario.

The future of the Hong Kong port's container operations has been the subject of intense speculation, with massive port development taking place in China leading many to be decidedly pessimistic about the future of the port. However, although growth in recent years has been more erratic than in the past, traffic through the port of Hong Kong has grown strongly enough for the port to regain and hold its title as the world's busiest container port.

> *Despite the growing challenge presented by ports in Shenzen and elsewhere in mainland China, Hong Kong has continued to grow at a healthy rate. The latest throughput count carried out by the Hong Kong Port and Maritime Board (HKPMB) indicates that in 2000 the port handled 18.1 million TEU, 11.7% more than in 1999.[21]*

The Hong Kong Port and Marine Board remains confident of the port's future as the principal outlet for the exports of Southern China, as is reported to expect 5 per cent per annum growth over the next five years, implying a total throughput of around 24 million TEU by 2006. This compares with a more conservative forecast in the present study of 20.0 million TEU in the same year.

The difference is due to differing views on how much impact the growth and development of other ports in China — and in particular the Shenzen ports — is likely to have on Hong Kong port volumes. Early statistics for 2001, which suggest a decline in Hong Kong port volumes in the first half of the current year, lend some credence to a more conservative approach, but with limited information as yet available it is difficult to disentangle the competitive effect of increase mainline calls at the Shenzen ports from the economic impact of the slowdown in the US economy. The latter is likely to be reversed as the world economy recovers; the former is not.

The MPPM estimates are that just over 5 million TEU of the Hong Kong port's total volume will be due to trans-shipment cargoes. It should be noted in this context that the MPPM definition of trans-shipment movements is somewhat different from that in the official port statistics. While the latter refers only to containers transferred from one ship to another within a dedicated container terminal, the MPPM definition refers to again cargo that arrives in the port of Hong Kong by ship or barge (including river trade) and also departs by ship or barge with the same cargo inside. It is thus more inclusive that the definition of the port statistics.

Figure 8-7 indicates that, while China cargoes continue to be by far the most important component of Hong Kong port's trans-shipment mix, they will not be as

---

[21] *Containerisation International*, July 2001.

dominant as they have traditionally been. This is consistent with the hypothesis that direct calls at the Shenzen ports in particular will capture a significant proportion of the cargoes traditionally trans-shipped over the port of Hong Kong. At the same time, both the 'base case' and the 'big ships' scenario envisage the emergence of Shanghai as a major alternative trans-shipment centre for China cargoes.

Apart from China cargoes, the main trans-shipment business of Hong Kong port in the model is as a relay centre for cargoes from South-East Asia and Oceania to North and Central America.

It should be noted, however, that both scenarios assume that cargoes from the principal ports of China will not be trans-shipped in Kaohsiung, Taichung or Keelung. Relaxation of this assumption would lead to a downward revision of the projected Hong Kong port volumes.

**Figure 8-7: Breakdown of forecast trans-shipment movements:
Port of Hong Kong – 2011 (base case)**

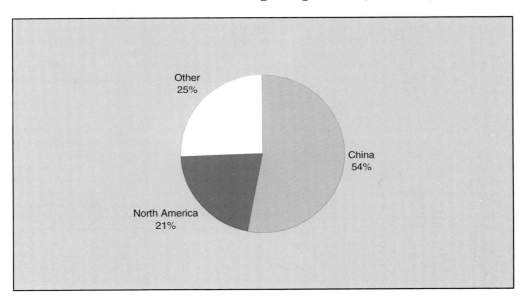

8.3.6 Shanghai

As noted above, both the 'base case' and 'big ships' scenario envisage that the planned deepwater trans-shipment hub at Shanghai will be fully operational by 2011.

Even without trans-shipment cargoes, Shanghai is expected to become a major world port by 2011. The MPPM estimates place the volume of origin-destination cargo through this port at over 11 million TEU by 2011. Provided current infrastructure constraints can by overcome, this massive base load will serve as an effective anchor for mainline ship calls to Shanghai, and provide the density of services that would provide the foundations for a substantial trans-shipment business.

Under the assumptions of the 'base case', this trans-shipment business is expected to grow to 7.7 million TEU by 2011. As Shanghai's hinterland volumes make it a leading contender for East Asian call on the streamlined services envisaged in the 'big ships' scenario, trans-shipment volumes in this scenario are even higher.

The trans-shipment business of Shanghai is focussed quite clearly on Chinese cargo, which is estimated to account for 85 per cent of all trans-shipment cargo through the port. The next largest component is the trans-shipment of Japanese cargoes, principally cargoes to or from Europe, which accounts for 6 per cent of the forecast total. The remaining 6 per cent is comprised of a miscellany of minor cargo movements to/from other countries.

**Figure 8-8: Breakdown of forecast trans-shipment movements:
Shanghai – 2011 (base case)**

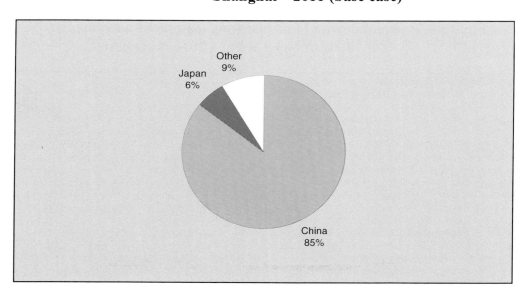

8.3.7 Busan and Gwangyang

The study forecasts place the total volume moving through these two ports in 2011 at 12.5 million TEU and 8.9 million TEU respectively in the 'base case'. Both suffer a minor reduction in trans-shipment volumes under the assumptions of the 'big ships' scenario, in which Busan's volume is estimated at 11.9 million and Gwangyang's at 8.8 million.

Trans-shipment at these two ports is discussed jointly as the ports are located within close proximity, and allocation of shipping services between the two is to a very large extent speculative. As this will in turn impact on the volume and distribution of trans-shipment cargoes at each of the port, analysis of trans-shipment patterns at the two ports combined in likely to be more meaningful than an analysis of each individually.

Total trans-shipment volume at the two ports is expected to be approximately 9 million TEU by 2011. It is clear from that, once again, cargo from Chinese ports will comprise the greater part of this volume: this cargo, mostly from the northern ports of China, accounts for approximately 65 per cent of total trans-shipment volume. Most the remaining volume is likely to be made up from other short sea feeder movements: from Japan, especially Kyushu and ports of the west coast, from North Korea, and domestic feeder services. Relay cargo movements are not expected to be significant.

**Figure 8-9: Breakdown of forecast trans-shipment movement:
Republic of Korea ports – 2011 (base case)**

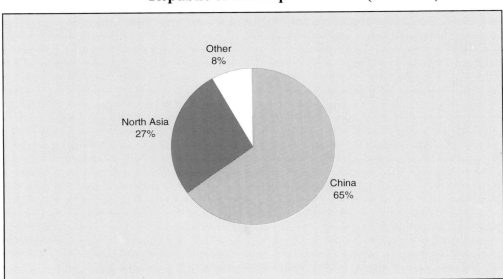

The forecasts of the MPPM model are somewhat lower than those currently adopted for planning purposes in the Republic of Korea. A key issue is the extent to which the ports of the Republic of Korea can establish and maintain a sustainable pricing and performance advantage over the ports of northern part of China. The range and quality of services mainline services to the key mainland destinations will clearly be critical to the future trans-shipment volumes at the Korean ports, and shipping line choices will be determined in part by port performance. If services to mainland ports are more limited than assumed in the 'base case' scenario, there is a chance that higher volumes could be realized. However, with initiatives such as the involvement of the PSA Corporation Ltd. in the development of the port of Dalian, it is likely to be difficult to maintain a significant price and quality advantage.

8.3.8   Japanese Ports

Total trans-shipment volumes at the Japanese hub ports in 2011 are estimated at approximately 1 million TEU. This is an increase of only around 40 per cent over 1999 volumes, and represents a significant decline in the relative importance of these ports as trans-shipment centres within the Asian liner shipping scene.

This forecast represents the continuation of a trend that have been going on for some time. As industrial activity within Asia has become more and more dispersed, the network of inter-continental shipping services, which was at one time concentrated almost exclusively on Japan, has gradually become more diffused and extensive, eliminating the previous need to trans-ship in Japan. At the same time, a range of new trans-shipment centres have developed at points closer to the origins and destinations of containerized cargo. The relatively high cost structure of Japanese ports has also been a disadvantage in competing for highly mobile trans-shipment cargoes. None of these factors is likely to later over the next decade.

9. CONTAINER BERTH REQUIREMENTS

The study estimates that the number of containers handled within the ESCAP region will more than double over the next decade. While there remains room for productivity improvements in some ports of the region, in many instances port productivity in Asian ports – as measured by throughput per metre of berth provided – in already very high. The expected increase in port throughput will therefore demand considerable investment in additional container berths.

The study attempts to estimate the number of berths that would be required. Estimating port capacity is a complex and often contentious issue, and precise estimates require the application of detailed simulation models and data on vessel arrival patterns and service times. Such detailed analysis is clearly beyond the scope of the present study. However, it is possible to obtain a good overall appreciation of the scale of the task that will be faced by port managers of the ESCAP region using a simple methodology. In general, the throughput that can be achieved per berth at a particular port will increase with the size of the average container exchange, the average size of ships visiting the port, and the level of port equipment. In general, there is a systematic correlation between the 'status' of the port and these factors: global hub ports tend to handle large ships discharging high box numbers at well-equipped terminals. Local ports tend to handle small, often semi-container ships discharging modest volumes of containers at multi-purpose berths. It is not difficult to derive reasonable indicative performance benchmarks for each type of port. Applying these benchmarks to the expected increase in container volumes provides a reasonable estimate of the number of additional berths that will be required over the next decade.

On the other hand, because berths at major hubs need to provide extensive land backing, deep water alongside the berth, and sufficient cranage to handle large volumes in a short period, the cost of providing an additional berth at such ports is generally higher.

For the purpose of estimating future berth requirements, ports were divided into five different classes, and an indicative throughput per berth and construction cost per berth assigned to ports in each class.

Table 9-1: Port classification and indicative throughput per berth

Port Class	Description	Throughput per berth	Indicative Cost per berth
1	World class hub port	350,000 TEU	US$80m
2	Major port with many mainline services	300, 000 TEU	US$60m
3	Important secondary port	250,000 TEU	US$60m
4	Feeder or regional port	200,000 TEU	US$40m
5	Minor port using multipurpose facilities	100,000 TEU	US$40m

The study estimates that, in total, 434 new container berths will be required to meet anticipated demand in 2011. The biggest share of this total is accounted for by China including Hong Kong, China and Taiwan Province of China, which will require over 160 new berths by the end of the decade. South-East Asia's requirements are 124 berths, of which Singapore alone will require around 43 berths. North Asia (excluding China) and South Asia will require 88 and 41 new berths, respectively.

Figure 9-1: Subregional shares of new container berth requirements (1999–2011)

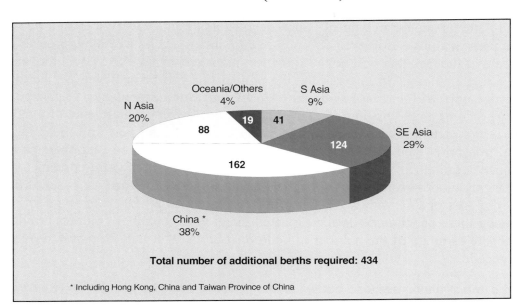

Obviously, this will entail very significant capital expenditure. Precise investment requirements will depend on the particular conditions that prevail at each new development site. However, based on typical costs to develop new infrastructure and procure the handling equipment required to allow the terminal to operate at a satisfactory level of efficiency, the total capital required has been estimated at approximately US$27 billion.

Figure 9-2 presents the study estimates of the capital investment required in the ESCAP region to meet the forecast demand for container port services over the next decade.

It should be noted that the costs presented in Figure 9-2 include only the cost of developing the terminals themselves. Substantial additional investment will also be required to secure adequate access to the terminals by road, rail and inland waterways, which will be essential for the effective distribution of containers to expanded port hinterlands. The additional costs of dredging, the provision of breakwaters and the establishment of land transport links and intermodal interchanges could easily double this total.

Figure 9-2: Estimated cost of additional berth provision by subregion

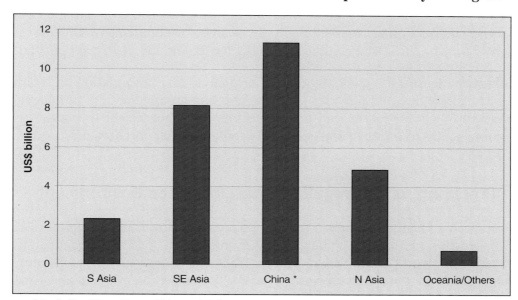

* Including Hong Kong, China and Taiwan Province of China

10. POLICY GUIDELINES

Within the context of the changing maritime environment and future prospects described in the previous chapters, there is an urgent need to review policies and implement more robust strategies if countries in the ESCAP region are to position their economies to meet the challenges of the next decade. In an increasingly competitive and globalized market place, the search for comparative advantage will inevitably focus on the cost and effectiveness of the export and import supply chain.

This chapter focuses on emerging issues critical to the formulation of maritime policies and strategies, and provides some insights and required actions at the national and regional levels for public and private sectors to be successful in providing and maintaining access to efficient and competitive shipping and port services.

10.1 Preparing for a Deregulated and Liberalized Environment

Maritime policy changes brought about by countries in the ESCAP region over the last two decades are part of a much broader movement towards deregulation and liberalization of world trade and industry. Policies in both the United States and Europe have been moving towards greater reliance on deregulated market mechanisms by limiting the scope of cooperative arrangements between shipping lines.

Perhaps more important for the ESCAP region, maritime transport services are included in the General Agreement on Trade in Services (GATS) within the multilateral framework of the World Trade Organization (WTO). During the Uruguay Round, international maritime transport was recognized to be already highly liberalized, and maritime auxiliary services and access to and use of port services were therefore included in the maritime schedule for discussion. The negotiations are due to resume within the WTO framework and may be extended beyond auxiliary services and ports to include aspects such as multimodal transport, inland waterways and the land transport leg of international maritime transport.

For countries in the region, particularly developing countries which are becoming increasingly reliant on shipping services provided by foreign fleets, it is of paramount importance to review policies and strategies to ensure that they can maintain access to efficient and competitive shipping services. At the same time, there is an increasing concern with respect to the impact of liberalization of maritime services on national shipping capabilities and the possibility that this may lead to the diminishing participation of countries in the region in the carriage of their sea-borne trade.

At the national level, countries could undertake detailed studies to review the new environment within which they should shape their maritime policies and strategies. Governments could collaborate with the public sector and private sector industry to review national positions with respect to the timing and sequencing of deregulation and liberalization.

At the regional level, an in-depth assessment of the possible impact of deregulation and liberalization of maritime services on national shipping fleets could be undertaken by regional and international organizations and agencies to assist countries in examining policies and strategies. Regional and subregional seminars could provide the opportunity for the exchange of experience and views on the latest developments in deregulation and liberalization, including WTO/GATS negotiations.

10.2 Identifying Niche Markets

The majority of ESCAP member countries seek to develop national shipping services to carry a portion of their external trade. However, in view of the size of the investments and extensive network required to participate in the global shipping port services, it is an increasing challenge for developing economies in the region to maintain competitiveness in the area of providing maritime services. There is therefore a need to identify and promote national flag carrier involvement in areas where there is comparative advantage or strategic necessity.

In an effort to contain costs, some of the major international shipping lines, many of whom are based in developed countries, "flag out" their ships to provide greater flexibility of operation and other fiscal advantages. In some countries in the region, the regulations and requirements, which sometimes include the imposition of duties and taxes, discourage companies from registering under the national flag.

At the national level, there is an urgent need to identify areas where developing country fleets have a comparative advantage or strategic necessity. In the container sector, possible opportunities for further growth include niche markets such as in the provision of feeder services or express shuttle services between a national port and single international destinations. An alternative or complementary approach could be to develop services in collaboration with international shipping operators.

Policy makers and industry could also critically review the viability of national flag fleets and the present levels of direct and indirect support provided by governments. The existing regulations and requirements, and particularly prevailing taxes and duties on shipping which operates in international services, need to be reviewed with a view to increasing the attractiveness of registration and the competitiveness of the national flag. In this process, governments should seek the assistance of the private sector with a view to exploring opportunities where national flag shipping can be successfully deployed and identifying policy and strategic requirements within the shipping sector and ways in which these could be achieved at minimum cost.

At the regional level, assistance should be given to countries in undertaking their reviews and opportunities be provided to share positive experience in the methodologies and processes applied. An analysis of the different registration regimes and direct and indirect support provided to national fleets by governments within and outside the region could be prepared as the basis for discussion and consideration of regional countries. Case studies of 'best practices' could also assist countries in formulating and implementing policies and strategies. A regional meeting of experts could provide opportunity for countries to share experience and information on successful strategies and to evaluate alternative proposals.

10.3 Prioritization of Port Development

With increased demands for capital investment in ports, prioritization of port development projects will become increasingly necessary to avoid uneconomical investment and to ensure that funds are available for essential port development projects. This will require resisting the temptation to use port development projects as a means of satisfying the political demands of local communities, and ensuring that the funds are applied to projects that will provide the highest social and economic return. Coordinated planning may be necessary in order to avoid wasteful investment in duplicated facilities.

At the national level, countries could prioritize national port development projects, taking into account their economic and social benefits and financial viability.

At the regional level, regional and international organizations and agencies could assist countries of the region in evaluating projects from an international perspective. Training programmes could be organized to assist member countries in enhancing capabilities for project evaluation and prioritization. Relatively simple software programmes such as the ESCAP/UNDP financial economic planning models could be disseminated to countries for application.

10.4 Private Sector Partnership

Faced with increased demands for capital investment in other sectors as well as in ports, it is unlikely that Government's will be either willing or be able to provide all of the capital required for future port developments. The private sector will need to provide a significant share of the total.

The past decade has seen many experiments with private sector investments in the port sector, which, in many ESCAP countries, has historically been the exclusive preserve of the public sector. Many of these experiments have been resounding successes in the ports in ESCAP countries. However, lack of transparency and continued resistance from labour have been cited as major obstacles to further private sector involvement. It may become more difficult to attract private capital in the future, as private investors become more discriminating in the choice of projects.

This will require Governments to develop more innovative incentives for private investment. The challenge will be to reconcile this need with the equally compelling need that countries maintain strategic control of their vital international transport links.

At the national level, governments, in collaboration with their financial institutions, could institutionalize a range of mechanisms for public-private partnerships, which offer varying levels of risk, resource inputs and ongoing involvement of the partners. For example, a joint venture, in which both the government and the private sector contribute assets, resources, technology, management and operational expertise, could ensure sharing of the related risks and benefits between public and private sector partners;

At the regional level, regional and country-level forums could help governments to exchange regional experiences of best practices in creating favourable public opinion with regard to private sector participation in ports.

10.5 Emphasis on Productivity

The port development task forecast in the previous chapter is clearly a challenging one. It is also a matter of great national importance. Unless port facilities are adequate to meet the expanded demand, the potential for economic growth through trade will be stifled.

It is clear that an increased focus on port productivity can reduce the need to invest significant quantities of new capital in expanding port facilities. Substituting productivity gains for new port development will have the additional advantage of avoiding the conflicts between environmental and economic objectives that will inevitably and increasingly accompany new port development.

At the national level, countries could review the productivity of their ports and identify major impediments.

At the regional level, a region-wide survey could be undertaken by regional and international organizations and agencies to assist countries in benchmarking the best models in port operation and management. Assistance could be provided to regional ports in applying information and communications technologies (ICT) to enhance port productivity, particularly through networking of regional ports in order to exchange data, information and software.

10.6 Intermodal Integration

The increased volumes of containers moving through the ports will place great stress on the land transport interface and generate a need for faster and more efficient intermodal connections to the hinterlands. At the same time, the demand of shippers for "seamless" logistics is likely to continue and intensify. There is an urgent need for ports to play a lead role in providing the necessary facilities for logistics growth.

At the national level, countries could review their transport and logistics systems to identify current bottlenecks in the national and regional transport and logistics chain and ensure the provision of efficient intermodal transport and logistics systems supported by high-quality infrastructure, particularly to expand port hinterlands;

At the regional level, regional and international organizations and agencies could provide assistance to member countries in developing integrated transport and logistics systems, which increasingly require sophisticated planning tools. Organizations and agencies could help countries of the region to forecast trade and capacity requirements for hinterland linkages.

READERSHIP SURVEY

The Transport, Communications, Tourism and Infrastructure Development Division of ESCAP is undertaking an evaluation of this publication/report. We would appreciate it if you could complete this questionnaire and return it, at your earliest convenience to

Director
Transport, Communications, Tourism and
Infrastructure Development Division
ESCAP, United Nations Building
Rajdamnern Nok Avenue, Bangkok 10200, THAILAND
Fax: (662) 02-280-6042

QUESTIONNAIRE

Title of the publication/report: Regional Shipping and Port Development Strategies Under a Changing Maritime Environment

Publication/report call number: ST/ESCAP/2153

	Excellent	Very Good	Average	Poor
A. Please indicate your assessment of the publication on:				
• presentation/format	4	3	2	1
• readability	4	3	2	1
• timeliness of information	4	3	2	1
• coverage of subject matter	4	3	2	1
• overall quality	4	3	2	1
B. How useful is the publication for your work ?				
• provision of information	4	3	2	1
• clarification of issues	4	3	2	1
• its findings	4	3	2	1
• overall usefulness	4	3	2	1

C. Suggestions for improving the publication/report:

_____

_____

_____

Your background information, please:

Name:..
Title/position:...
Institution/Organization:...
Office Address: ....
....
....

Thank you for your kind cooperation in completing this questionnaire.